TO COME
TO LIFE
MORE FULLY

AN EAST WEST JOURNEY

TO COME TO LIFE MORE FULLY

AN EAST WEST JOURNEY

JOHN GREENFELDER SULLIVAN

TRADITIONAL ACUPUNCTURE INSTITUTE, INC.

COLUMBIA, MARYLAND

Published in the United States of America

The author is grateful to Frederick Franck for permission to reprint his Oxherding Pictures, to the late John Levering for the symbol that appears on the cover, and to Joe Robertson for the back cover photograph.

Cover design by Betsey Heuisler and Mary Ellen Zorbaugh

Library of Congress Cataloging-in-Publication Data:
Sullivan, John Greenfelder.
    To come to life more fully : an East-West journey / John Greenfelder Sullivan.
        p. cm.
    Includes bibliographical references.
    ISBN 0-912381-01-9 (pbk.)
    1. Philosophy, Comparative. 2. Philosophy, Chinese.
3. Self (Philosophy) 4. Process philosophy. I. Title.
B799.S85 1991   91-40508
100—dc20   CIP

To

HELEN, GREGG AND HEATHER

for the life we share

CONTENTS

PART TWO

LIFE AS ENERGY
The World in Cyclic Motion

PART THREE

LIFE AS DWELLING
The World as Seven Domains

PART FOUR

LIFE AS HEALING SERVICE

Returning to the Source

ACKNOWLEDGMENTS

The aim of this work is
to come to life more fully
so as to serve life more wisely and more nobly:
sageliness within; kingliness without.

The above is the stated purpose of a program for adult learners called SOPHIA—the School of Philosophy and Healing in Action.[1] The formulation is mine — an attempt to speak anew the ancient Chinese adage: "sageliness within; kingliness without."

In the SOPHIA project, we begin thus: before the participants introduce themselves, we do the exercise of the bow. Carried out in circles of six or eight, the exercise is a simple one: one person steps into the circle and bows to each of his or her fellow members, one by one. Then the next person makes the round, until all have had a turn. The exercise is done in silence, with reverence and care.

The bow is a way of honoring the wholeness within, a way of acknowledging the core of who we are and the source that joins us to all beings. This center has many names: our original nature, the kingdom within, the Buddha-nature, the Christ-nature, the Spirit, the Source. In India, there is a word *namaste* which accompanies the bow. Some years ago, I came across the following beautiful explanation of what this word means:

> In India, when we meet, we often say *namaste*,
> which means, I honor the place in you where the
> entire universe lives. I honor the place in you of
> love, of light, of truth, of peace. I honor the place
> in you, where, if you are in that place in you, and
> I am in that place in me, there is only one of us.

We begin in an atmosphere of deep acknowledgment. We bow and are bowed to, giving and receiving in turn. In this spirit, I invite you to an East-West inquiry into life and learning, health and healing. Together, in mutuality of presence and participation, we can discover (or rediscover) *that which matters*.

I introduce myself by bowing to you. If you open a space of respectful listening, then you will accept what I share as an invitation to further discovery. You will remember for me when I forget; you will improve my words when I speak haltingly and poorly.

Who am I, the one who speaks to you? How can I show you who I am and from whence I come? Perhaps, by a series of bows, a set of acknowledgments.

I acknowledge the place I was born: Newport, Rhode Island, a city by the sea, rich in history from colonial times. From here, I take my sense of place, my citizenship in a city, my earliest feeling for history. Though I knew little of the native Americans who were the first people to dwell here, I knew, at least, their words. I knew we lived on the island of Aquidneck, between the Sakonnet River and Narragansett Bay. Something earlier and deeper still was given me: an abiding love of the sea. For all these gifts from the sea, I express gratitude.[2]

I honor my parents, John Joseph Sullivan and Helen Marion Greenfelder, who were also born in Newport. I honor my sister, Elaine, and a wider web of aunts, uncles and cousins. I bow to my grandmothers, born of Irish immigrants who settled in Newport, and my two grandfathers, who were themselves immigrants — one Irish and one Swiss. My people came to this land over a broad ocean with little money but very great dreams. The Statue of Liberty and its inscription were still fresh for them.

The Newport that I knew was an Irish-Catholic Newport. Though I walk along that path no longer, I entered deeply into this faith and dwelled long within it before leaving it. From that tradition, I acknowledge receiving a sense of the contemplative life, of sacramental reality, a feeling for the great religious centers in Europe, an understanding of the comradeship of men, and those magic times and places where liturgies briefly revealed something of the depth of life. Early on, I remember the evening when I first heard the Benedictine monks of the Portsmouth Priory chanting *Tenebrae* as the fog rolled in and dissolved the world. Early on, I remember a time on Warwick Neck in Rhode Island. In the stillness of a chill Holy Saturday night, the new fire blazed up from its place on the outside portico of a chapel in full sight of the Pascal moon shining across the bay. For such nourishment, I bow deeply.

A life has many strata. I call to mind earlier strata of my life by acknowledging Don Russell, Paul Crowley, and Linda Votta Sullivan. Each evokes a time, a place, a life.

For some twenty years now, I have lived in the gently rolling Piedmont plateau of North Carolina. In coming to North Carolina, I was also returning to a first love, philosophy. I came to teach at a small college called Elon, a place whose name comes from the Hebrew word for "oak tree." Here, in North Carolina, I acknowledge many teachers and colleagues who have enriched my teaching and learning. Among these are Maynard Adams, David Falk, and their colleagues at the University of North Carolina in Chapel Hill; Ferris Reynolds, Bruce Waller, Martha Smith, John Alweynse, Russell Gill and my many other friends at Elon; Bolton Anthony, David Purpel, and others in Greensboro. For giving me good breakfasts, a place to write and numberless cups of coffee, I also express gratitude to Bobbie King and all the folks at Pete's Grill in Gibsonville.

My Irish ancestors lived and worked beside the Atlantic on the Irish coast. I have lived and worked along the Atlantic seaboard of the United States from Rhode Island to the Carolinas. These elements come together in the three women to whom I dedicate this book: my mother, Helen Greenfelder Sullivan; my wife and love, Gregg Winn Sullivan; and my daughter, Heather Anne Votta Sullivan. For these three, words fail. I bow profoundly and most gratefully.

It remains to situate a theme which will be evident in this work. For the past twenty years, my interests — philosophical, psychological, and religious — have converged along an Eastern way of seeing and being. This treasure may be acknowledged by making three additional bows.

First, I bow to two people who are mentors and friends: the artist and author Frederick Franck and his wife, Claske. From Frederick, I came to see that playful, often irreverent, humor dwells with the deepest sense of life. Like Frederick, I am drawn to speak two languages — East and West; to speak of communion in the image of the tea ceremony and the tea ceremony as sacrament. With Frederick, I understand that, for the mystics anyway, East and West are "not one, not two." From Claske, I have learned to see with new eyes the lines of the old Shaker song, Simple Gifts: "When true simplicity is gained, to bow and to bend we will not be ashamed. To turn, to turn, 'twill be our delight, until turning, turning, we come round right."

Second, I bow to a community of friends and colleagues: those who have come together around the Traditional Acupuncture Institute (TAI) in Columbia, Maryland. I bow to my old friends, Bob Duggan and Dianne Connelly, who founded this remarkable center. I bow to my Columbia teaching partner, Julia Measures, with whom I designed the SOPHIA program in close collaboration with Bob, Dianne and Mary Ellen Zorbaugh. I acknowledge Charlotte Kerr, Haig Ignatius, Cyrie Barnes, Jack Daniel, Jim McCormick and many others on the TAI faculty and staff, as well as Larry Daloz, Lynne Battaglia, Woody Beville, Fritz Smith and my other fellow TAI Board members past and present. Also, I am grateful to Susan Duggan for her gracious hospitality and abiding care and to the members of the SOPHIA classes for support and encouragement. For bringing this work into print I thank Mary Ellen Zorbaugh, Guy Hollyday, Laura Klein and Susan Hyde and Linda Martindale.

My last bow is to the ecologist Thomas Berry, with whom I had contact for less than a day. I choose him to stand for all those persons who have touched my life however briefly and given me the gifts or blows I have needed to go forward. The story is this: in the spring of 1988, Thomas Berry, a native of Greensboro, North Carolina, returned home to give a workshop at UNC-Greensboro on "Education in an Ecological Age." That semester, I was spending a mini-sabbatical with friends in the School of Education at UNC-Greensboro. I was also overseeing the pilot year of the SOPHIA project in Columbia, Maryland. My thinking and reading spanned diverse areas: education, ecology, developmental psychology, Creation Spirituality, Confucian philosophy and the poetry of Rumi. I only knew Thomas Berry as the character "Thomas" in Brian Swimme's *The Universe Is a Green Dragon*.[3] The real Thomas Berry was an unlikely, grandfatherly prophet, who mentioned, in passing, how similar the ancient worldview of China was to the emerging ecological worldview. After the lecture, I learned, to my delight, that Thomas Berry was a student of Chinese thought. He graciously sent me his papers on China. A serendipitous connection was shared and themes in my own thinking came together. I had found a way of bringing together two major strands: what I now call the seven domains and the healing processes which are evident in SOPHIA. Sharing these insights is what my book is about.

Notes

[1] SOPHIA, the School of Philosophy and Healing In Action, is a program for adult learners offered by The Traditional Acupuncture Institute, Inc., American City Building, Suite 100, Columbia, Maryland, 21044. This program explores the practical Chinese philosophy that undergirds health and healing. In the first-year program, eight intensive weekends are devoted to principles of energetics and diagnostic skills so that participants may expand their vision and contribute more effectively in personal, societal and global domains.

[2] This phrase is meant to acknowledge Anne Morrow Lindbergh's beautiful book, *Gift From the Sea* (New York: Pantheon Books, 1955).

[3] See Brian Swimme, *The Universe Is a Green Dragon* (Santa Fe, NM: Bear and Company, 1984).

PART ONE

LIFE AS EXPLORATION

Learning from the Earth

THE IMAGE: "OCEAN-EARTH" FROM SPACE

For centuries, we have seen the moon from the viewpoint of the earth. Only in our time have we seen the earth from the viewpoint of the moon. The shift of standpoints is immense.

On July 20, 1969, the Apollo 11 Mission placed a man on the moon. From this mission and others like it, we have photographs of the earth from space. Hauntingly beautiful photographs show our planet *as a whole*, enveloped by its swirling, cloud-carrying atmosphere — a blue-green planet blessed with water in abundance. Indeed, nearly three quarters of Earth's surface is covered with water. As Arthur C. Clarke has commented: "How inappropriate to call this planet Earth, when clearly it is Ocean."[1]

Dean Francis B. Sayre paints a word picture of

> this fragile miracle of life;
> spinning blue in the sea of black;
> precious beyond compare;
> sacred in its wondrous possibility. [2]

Less than a year later, on April 22, 1970, we witnessed the first Earth Day celebration. Now, over twenty years later, we are more and more learning old lessons anew. The Earth is Mother. The Earth is Teacher.

The Earth is Healer.

The Earth is an intermediary reality — fathered and mothered by greater cosmic forces. As the ancient Chinese remind us, we humans are an intermediary reality, existing as we do between the heavens and the earth. Thus, say the ancient teachings, the world is a mirror to us and we to it.

Ecologist and China-scholar, Thomas Berry, again and again stresses the primacy of earth as a creative, self-sustaining reality. For example, he writes that . . .

> the earth is itself
> the primary physician,
> primary lawgiver,
> primary revelation of the divine,
> primary scientist,
> primary technologist,
> primary commercial venture,
> primary artist,
> primary educator, and
> primary agent in whichever other activity
> we find in human affairs.[3]

Thus, in taking the Earth as Mother, as Teacher, as Healer, we are following insights both ancient and new.

In the Chinese tradition, what we call Planet Earth would be spoken of as the Great Parents, Heaven and Earth. This is because the manifest world is ever in the dance of polarity, of yin and yang. An image of the heavens and the earth can be seen in the figure of the square within the circle. Old Chinese coins are round (signifying the heavens) with a square cut out of the center (signifying the earth). Imagine an astronaut on the moon looking through an ancient Chinese coin at the planet which is our home. Realize that the planet is to be seen less as a thing, more as a process of life unfolding. Life arises between the heavens and the earth, the ancients would say. The earth itself is a living organism — Gaia, some of our contemporaries are saying.[4] Ancient Chinese sages and modern Western scientists share the insight that our world is a living web of interconnected, self-regulating life.

How can we approach such life within life? In this work, I shall approach life in a fourfold manner: *life as exploration, life as energy, life as dwelling, life as healing service.* Taking the earth as teacher is a reminder that we are always in an inquiry — an inquiry concerning ourselves, others and the world we share.

Part One — *Life as Exploration* — introduces an approach that is cross-cultural, cross-epochal, and transpersonal. The method is cross-cultural, moving from West to East and back. The method is cross-epochal, moving from new timeframes to old and back.[5] The method is transpersonal, moving from outer to inner and back, from kingliness to sageliness and back. Such a movement takes us beyond the individual to serve larger communions, beyond the lifetime through wider times to the mystery within and beyond all time.[6]

Part One — *Life as Exploration* — has three chapters. Chapter One presents our inquiry as global in scope, suggesting a circumnavigation of the earth both spatial (East and West) and temporal (old and new). Chapter Two anchors the comparative method in ancient Chinese wisdom. Two sages, Lao Tzu and Confucius — like yin and yang, like inner and outer — act as guides on a path to wholeness. Finally, Chapter Three explains the fourfold structure of the work: (i) *Life as Exploration*, (ii) *Life as Energy*, (iii) *Life as Dwelling*, and (iv) *Life as Healing Service*.

Thus, Part One gives instructions on how we shall proceed, introduces two guides and offers a preview of where we shall be going. Just as the old Chinese coin represents earth as a square within the circle of the heavens, so our fourfold structure exists within a circle and creates a circular motion: making us aware that exploring life — as energy and as dwelling — is for the sake of healing service; making us aware that healing service — to life as dwelling and energy — requires ongoing exploration. All this is carried out under the image of the earth seen as a whole, in the service of life as it unfolds in space and time between the heavens and the earth.

Notes

1 Quoted in J. E. Lovelock, *Gaia: A New Look at Life on Earth* (Oxford, England: Oxford University Press, 1st pub. 1979; rev. ed. 1987), p. 84.

2 These are the words of Dean Sayre on the occasion of the dedication of the Washington Cathedral's "space window" in which is preserved a rock from the moon. Quoted in Kenneth Gatland, *An Illustrated Encyclopedia of Space Technology* (New York: Salamander Harmony Books, 1981), p. 106.

³ See Berry, *The Dream of the Earth* (San Francisco: Sierra Club Books, 1988), p. 107.

⁴ See J. E. Lovelock, *Gaia*.

⁵ In chapter nine on the cultural domain, I note five cultural epochs. At this juncture, "old and new" is a shorthand for ranging over all the epochs of the human story.

⁶ The term "transpersonal" has arisen to characterize attempts to present developmental psychology as continuous with those higher states of consciousness that are mapped by the mystics and sages. The dialectic between sageliness within (especially Lao Tzu) and kingliness without (especially Confucius) as well as my treatment of the domains insures such an inclusive intent, without having to adopt either Piagetian or Jungian stage theory. For a fuller discussion of these more standard approaches to the transpersonal, see Michael Washburn, *The Ego and the Dynamic Ground: A Transpersonal Theory of Human Development* (Albany, NY: State University of New York Press, 1988) and also Ken Wilber, *The Atman Project: A Transpersonal View of Human Development* (Wheaton, IL: Theosophical Publishing Quest Books, 1980).

CHAPTER ONE

RESPECTING THE WORLD: EAST AND WEST, OLD AND NEW

Whoever discovered water, it wasn't the fish!

Imagine a cartoon-like fish who has spent life up to now swimming around. Imagine an immensely speeded up evolution. The fins become legs; the gills adapt to air; the fish pokes a head out of the water and starts to experience land. Suddenly, there is a preview of other animals in the realm of land as well as birds and other flying things in the realm of air. Indeed, as the fish looks up, she sees the creatures of land and of air. Now, it would be possible for our cartoon-like fish to become reflective. "So," she might say, " I have been in water; I have been swimming in a pond. I know this because I can compare water to land and earth to sky."

We too dwell in a world of "realities" structured by our collective thinking and acting, our shared expectations and evaluations. Without a contrast, we are no better than the unawakened fish. Without a contrast, we can neither describe nor assess "that in which we swim."

A. ASSUMPTIONS AND ALTERNATIVES

The great philosopher Plato told a story of prisoners condemned to dwell in a cave in circumstances much like a modern movie house.[1] Chained in place, their necks braced so they can only direct their vision to what is happening on the "screen," they are presumably happy. They know no other reality; they are prevented from having any point of comparison. All share a collective fiction and count it as "the real world."

Such are the conditions of their imprisonment.

One day, there is an intervention from without. One of the prisoners is taken to the world outside the cave — our world. Only then can the prisoner see that there is a better way, a fuller reality, a more beautiful mode of being. In the light of this alternative, the prisoner comes to understand his previously taken-for-granted life. It is as if he has awakened from a dream.

Filled with the joy of knowing such fuller reality, the awakened prisoner returns to "the cave." But, as occurs when one goes from bright sunlight into a darkened theatre, the prisoner's eyes take time to readjust to darkness. Unable to identify the shadow shapes that flicker across the cave wall "screen," the prisoner seems poorly adjusted. As he reports his experience of reality to his fellow prisoners, they think him deluded, perhaps mad. Finally, the cave-dwellers tell him — chillingly — that if he disturbs them further, they will kill him!

Plato's story forms a circle — a liberative movement from darkness to light and a compassionate return from the light to the darkness. Plato means the story as an analogy. We who tend to believe we have escaped from delusion are told a cutting truth: *We are the prisoners. What we label "the real world" is the cave.* The implications are breathtaking. If our world is the cave, then our collective illusions are what we mistake for truth, our collective addictions what we mistake for the good and our distorted dreams what we mistake for the beautiful. How can we awaken from this communal, hypnotic, daylight dream? How can we be liberated from our subtle, unfelt bonds?

The answer, as Plato in the West and the Buddha in the East realize, is a process. Such a process will distinguish between *content* and the *framework* we use to interpret the content. Content refers to the objects we become intrigued with (like the characters on the screen). Our interpretive framework is specified by the collective taken-for-granteds in which we dwell (like the entire cave). To bring the cave to light *as a cave* requires that in some way we go beyond it. To bring to light assumptions requires that we seek alternatives.

All this returns us to the need for comparatives — the fish in the pond needed a contrast; the prisoner needed to glimpse an alternative. Goethe once said that he who knows but one language knows no language. Max Muller, the great student of religion, took the idea one step further. One who knows one religion, he said, knows no religion. The point is clear: To see what is central, we need a contrast.

For our purposes, we need a strong contrast as regards both space and time. The contrast between East and West insures suitable diversity across space. But on a planet so Americanized, it is not enough to compare, say, modern Europe or North America with contemporary China and Japan. All tend to operate out of a shared industrial, technological paradigm. The contrast would be stronger if we compare a traditional (e.g. classical) time period in the East with our modern epoch (since the Renaissance) in the West.

B. WORLDVIEWS: IDEAL, DEFECT AND REMEDY

What do we find when we look at the major mythic stories of East and West? How can we begin to feel their similarities and differences?

Let us begin with the generic scheme of ideal/defect/remedy.[2] To illustrate, I will first use imagery and later speak of differences in languaging. First, the images:

In the West, the religions of the Book — Judaism, Christianity and Islam — all share respect for the Old Testament. The first image will come from Genesis: the image of being in a garden.

This is the *ideal*, given under an image: *being in a garden* — where the garden is a condition of at-one-ment, of life lived in obedience to the plan of God.

Since the ideal is understood as the plan of God imaged as a garden, the *defect* is imaged as a fall from that state, an exile from the garden. We look around and realize that we are not in such a unitive state. In fact, we are out of harmony with ourselves, estranged from others, cut off from nature and forgetful of our common origin.

Still, all is not lost: there is a *remedy*, a path from the defect to the ideal, a way to the Way, a possibility of return. In Joni Mitchell's famous 1960s song "Woodstock," she sang: "We are stardust. We are golden. And we've got to get ourselves back to the garden." Always the remedy is a journey from defect to ideal, a way back to the Way.

The remedy or return is understood differently in the separate traditions. The return may be through following Moses and the Torah, or Jesus and his Sermon on the Mount, or the Prophet Mohammed and the practices set forth in the Koran. Still, in all these Western views, the remedy is a journey from sin to salvation, from disunion to reunion — a return to the garden.

As a second example, consider Buddhism. Here the defect is imaged as the state of being asleep; the ideal is imaged as the state of being awake; and the remedy is instruction in meditation so as to move from being asleep (the defect) to being awake (the ideal).

It is said that there are eighty thousand ways of being asleep and eighty thousand ways of awakening. A true master — an awakened one — can instruct in meditation and, with skillful means, point the way for each sleeper to awaken.

C. CONTRASTING THE LANGUAGE OF EAST AND WEST

The ideal/defect/remedy pattern applies to ancient philosophies and religions both East and West. But the notion of the ideal is languaged and understood quite differently. Here, we will make the contrast sharper by comparing the modern West and the ancient East.

In the modern West, the ideal is often pictured as in the future, as not-yet-present possibility that will become real only if and when humans actualize it. Thus, the ideal is *not* thought of as the real. The real is the world as it *is* in the present; real = defect = present. The ideal is the world as it *ought to be*, a world that is set in an unreal future; ideal = unreal = future.

Notice the type of language used: the distinction is between is and ought, between *things as they are* — the defect, and *things as they ought to be, but are not yet* — the ideal. An example of this may be found in Western world religions as they are often conceptualized in modern times.[3] There is the plan of God (how things ought to be but are not) and there is the result of the Fall (things as they are but ought not be). Under this languaging, the movement from *what is* to *what ought to be* — from defect to ideal — takes on the features of striving, of effort, of will, of repenting and resolving to do better.

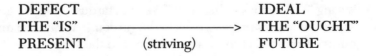

DEFECT		IDEAL
THE "IS"	——————>	THE "OUGHT"
PRESENT	(striving)	FUTURE

In the East, the language of "is vs. ought" is not preferred; rather the defect and the ideal are both seen as *what is* — but on different levels.[4] Provisionally,[5] we might distinguish between *how things are at the surface* (the defect) and *how things are at the depth* (the ideal). Notice that under this formulation, the ideal *is* the real. Also the ideal, which is truly real, is already and always *present* beneath or beyond the surface illusions. What I take myself to be (my identification with the surface

---

content of my life) is not what I truly am at my depth. At my depth, I am at one with the *context* of my life. On such an understanding, to go *from defect to ideal* is more like waking up than making New Year's resolutions, more like letting go of obstacles and illusory identifications than striving for what one does not have. At the surface level, there is disharmony; at the depth, one has never been other than what one was meant to be.

WHAT IS — ON SURFACE (EVERYDAY) LEVEL —
THE PRESENT — DEFECT

Process of letting go
of obstacles

WHAT IS — ON DEPTH (CORE BEING) LEVEL —
THE PRESENT — IDEAL

Here is an example. Imagine that you and I, along with many brothers and sisters, are the sons and daughters of a great King and Queen. Suppose that we live in a distant kingdom. Time passes and all of us princes and princesses become bored. We decide to produce a drama in which we will all have parts to play. In the play, some choose to play common folk; some, lords and ladies. Some of us choose to play statesmen or soldiers, priests or prostitutes, merchants or thieves, for all of the roles of life are represented. Since the kingdom has great resources, we are able to produce our play, not on a stage, but in a certain area of the kingdom. No effort is spared; each actress and actor is provided with all of the possessions of her or his character — clothes, houses, land, even mementos from the constructed past. Soon, the roles become so real and the play so serious that we, the actors, forget that we are only acting a part. At this point, we are living an illusion, a play that is no longer playful. We are embedded in roles with which we have identified. We forget that we are all brothers and sisters of royal lineage.

In similar fashion, the East can say: you are not who you think you are. You are more than the sum of your surface identities. You are these, yes. And you are also something more — at the core. You are in disharmony and yet there is also a sense in which you have never ceased to be exactly who and what you were meant to be.

D. The Contrasts Reviewed

Let us review the contrasts step by step. First, the ideal and defect are languaged differently.

	IDEAL		DEFECT
WESTERN language:	"what OUGHT to be"	vs.	"what IS"
EASTERN language:	"what IS at depth"	vs.	"what IS at surface"

Next, the West tends to place the ought (=ideal) in the future, the is (=defect) in the present. Finally, in the West, the defect is correlated with the real and the ideal is correlated with the not-real.

By contrast, the Eastern formulation utilizes not the language of is vs. ought but rather (at least, provisionally) the language of surface vs. depth. This tends to unfold as a double *is*: what *is* at the surface and what *is* at the depth.

There are at least two implications of framing the defect vs. ideal in the language of surface *is* vs. depth *is*:

First, because *both* the surface and the depth are co-present, one need not speak of coming to gain or get the ideal. The ideal is always and already present, as the depth of the ocean is always and already present even if one forgets the calm below when there are storms above. The ideal, for the Eastern masters, is not something which lies in the future; it is close at hand, present and available here and now. (So too are the surface phenomena present here and now.)

Second, whereas in the modern Western formula, the defect = the real, in the ancient Eastern formula, the ideal = the most real. The real world is preeminently that which springs from the depth dimension.

Since the ideal and defect are conceived differently in West and East, these differences will affect how the remedy is conceived.

In the West, the passage from Defect to Ideal
    is the passage from Is to Ought
    is the passage from present to future.

Hence, the remedy tends to be seen as a form of striving, of effort, of struggle, of will and commitment, like New Year's resolutions.

In the East, the passage from Defect to Ideal
    is the passage from Surface to Depth
    from what is *already present at the surface*
    to what is *already present at the depth.*

Hence, the remedy tends to be seen as a form of letting go, of shedding obstacles to the emergence of what was present all along.

Michelangelo was once asked how he created such marvelous statues. "It is easy," he replied. "You simply have to find a block of marble with the figure inside and then chip away whatever does not belong to it." Such is the Eastern way.

Notes

[1] See Edith Hamilton and Huntington Cairns, eds., *The Collected Dialogues of Plato*, Bollingen Series LXXI (Princeton, NJ: Princeton University Press, 1961), *The Republic*, Book VII. In Plato's version, above and behind the prisoners and unseen by them, there are puppeteers (with hand puppets). Behind and above the passageway of the puppeteers, there is a fire. The fire casts shadows of the puppets on the cave wall "screen." For the prisoners, this — being all they know — is the real world.

[2] I first came across this device in John E. Smith, *Experience and God* (New York: Oxford University Press, 1968).

[3] The mystics whether Christian, Jewish or Islamic often see matters differently. They speak and think in a mode much more like that of the ancient East.

[4] In chapter thirteen, I shall return to these themes and contend that, given the sense "ought" has in modern Western ethics, both Confucius and Lao Tzu are "ought-aversive."

[5] I say "provisionally" because we are still speaking here in dualistic terms. The deepest insights of the East go beyond all dualisms.

TWO ANCIENT GUIDES ON A PATH TO WHOLENESS

Everyone is a Confucian in public life,
a Taoist, in retirement.[1]

The earth turns and we experience day and night. In the day, we are active; in the night, we rest. We move out into the world; we move back into our home place. Such is the rhythm of our common life. Thus, there is public life and retirement every day.

The ancient Chinese also speak of "sageliness within; kingliness without." *(Sheng nei; wang wai.)* The rhythm is the same — contemplative stillness alternating with noble, generous-spirited action. Once again, two aspects of an integral life.

At the roots of ancient Chinese culture, two figures stand out: Lao Tzu (The Old Master) who stands at the origin of the Taoist tradition and Confucius (Master K'ung) who stands at the origin of the Confucian tradition. Throughout this work, these two shall be our principal guides.

In chapter one, I presented ancient Eastern thought in a general fashion and in service of uncovering assumptions. In this chapter and hereafter, I place the focus on the ancient Chinese classics (Confucian and Taoist). I do this for several reasons. First, such classical Chinese thinking has worth in its own right. Second, as Thomas Berry has pointed out, among the religions and philosophies of the classical epoch, the Chinese world view resonates most consistently with the emerging ecological world view.[2] What makes such ancient writings "classic" is that they plumb the human condition deeply; they speak to seekers across cultures and epochs, and allow us to discover (or rediscover) profound possibilities. What makes ancient Chinese wisdom especially attractive is that it speaks so well to our present, pressing needs.

A. BACKGROUND TO THE CHINESE CLASSICS

The Chinese classics lie at the source of one of the world's most remarkable cultures. Here, we are speaking of origins, and, when speaking of beginnings, the best course is to follow the way of myth and story.

The story of China begins in the mists of time — before 2000 B.C. when, it is said, China was ruled by the Sage Kings of the legendary Hsia dynasty.[3] Among these Sage Kings are Huang Ti (the Yellow Emperor) associated with silk, ceramics, healing and writing; Yao, given credit for the calendar, ritual, and music; and Shun, an adopted son renowned for filial devotion.

By 1500 B.C., the Shang dynasty was in place; by 1000 B.C., the mandate of heaven had passed to the Chou dynasty whose founding figures — King Wen, King Wu, and the Duke of Chou — are lauded as models of wise rule. So goes the story, and, if we move forward once again, we will meet at 500 B.C. the storyteller, Confucius (K'ung Ch'iu or, more popularly, K'ung Tzu — Master K'ung).

Confucius lived from about 551 B.C. to 479 B.C. Let us introduce Confucius in his early fifties in the year 500 B.C. The year 500 B.C. reminds us that Confucius is a contemporary of Siddhartha Gautama (b. 563 B.C.), who became the Buddha in distant India and who was a contemporary of the pre-Socratic philosophers of ancient Greece.

At the time of Confucius, China was in a feudal period dominated by a hereditary warrior aristocracy — a king and regional lords. Confucius' dream was of uniting China through common culture and shared heritage. Thus, Confucius and his school came to praise the five classics of Chou times:

(i) *The Book of Changes* (I-Ching)
(ii) *The Book of Songs* (Shih-Ching)
(iii) *The Book of Rituals* (Li-Ching)
(iv) *The Book of History* (Shu-Ching) and
(v) *The Spring and Autumn Annals* (Ch'un-ch'iu) — which chronicles events from 722 to 481 B.C. from the viewpoint of the state of Lu.

The most influential follower of Confucius was born a century after Master K'ung had died. That disciple was Mencius or Meng Tzu (Master Meng) who lived about 372-290 B.C.

In the Han dynasty (c. 202 B.C. – A.D. 220), China became a Confucian state, in part by developing a civil service chosen by merit examination based on the subjects taught in a newly formed national university. The curriculum of that university was the Five Classics presented above. Later would be added the Four Confucian Books (or the Books of the Four Philosophers):

(a) *The Analects* (Lun Yu) — material gathered on the teaching of Master K'ung (Confucius)
(b) *The Mencius* (Meng Tzu) — the writings of Mencius
(c) *The Doctrine of the Mean* (Chung Yung) — attributed to the grandson of Confucius
(d) *The Great Learning* (Ta Hsueh) — attributed to a disciple of Confucius

Both *The Doctrine of the Mean* and *The Great Learning* are embedded in *The Book of Rituals* and hence are part of both lists.

B. THE TWO GUIDES: CONFUCIUS AND LAO TZU

Classical Chinese thought has the ability *to hold opposites in creative harmony*. To appreciate this, we need only return to our anchor in time — 500 B.C. As soon as we bring Confucius on stage, we must bring a second figure on stage with him, the mysterious Old Master, Lao Tzu, to whom is attributed the *Tao Te Ching* or *Classic* (Ching) of the *Virtue/Power* (Te) of the *Way* (Tao).

About the magnificent *Tao Te Ching* and its author, controversy abounds. For our purposes, it is appropriate to retell the legend which makes Lao Tzu (the Old Master), an older contemporary of Confucius. Whatever the literal truth may be, the legend speaks a profound symbolic truth.

Confucius and his followers concern themselves with human culture (with its powerful myths and rituals), human history and heritage, and the training of leaders for public service. Confucius is a man of the city and, even more, a master of the ceremonies of good governance. Lao Tzu and his Taoist followers concern themselves with the natural world of the cloud-hidden mountains and forest streams, simple gifts and simplified living. Lao Tzu is, in effect, a mountain man and a master who listens to and learns from the deep rhythms of nature's way.

Since the natural world is indeed older than the human world, it is appropriate to make Lao Tzu older than Confucius. Confucius and Lao Tzu introduce two strands of classical Chinese thought. (The third strand enters later when the thought of the third contemporary, the Buddha, enters China.) For now, Lao Tzu and K'ung Tzu stand together — a complementary, though odd, couple. The Chinese prize the wisdom of both as is evident in the saying quoted earlier: "Everyone is a Confucian in public life and a Taoist in retirement."

The chart on the following page presents the complementary approaches of the two great sages.

In chapter one, we met two polarities: East and West; old and new. With this chapter, I have specified further, taking ancient China as our model for the wisdom of the East. In ancient China, we meet yet a third polarity: at the heart of this tradition, two teachers — Lao Tzu and K'ung Tzu — stand side by side. The first emphasizes the country; the second, the city. Lao Tzu primarily tells a story of nature; Confucius primarily tells a story of human culture. Both teachers, however, place the human within nature and nature within the human. Lao Tzu stresses "sageliness within"; Confucius stresses "kingliness without." Both teachers, however, have a practical intent, a healing purpose; both point to life. Together, they call us "to come to life more fully so as to serve life more wisely and more nobly." Together, they remind us of both sides of life: "Sageliness within; kingliness (or sovereign service) without."

C. A FURTHER NOTE ON HEALING AND WHOLENESS

Classical Chinese thought seeks neither to escape the world nor redeem the world. Instead it studies life — life arising and unfolding in the natural/human world. Life arises and unfolds between the heavens and the earth; life is taken to be the best guide. Classical Chinese thinking is, in the words of one writer, "polar-complete" rather than "fragmentary-absolute."[4] For example, the Chinese word *zhi* means both "to govern" and "to heal." The good scholar-official is also a good healer. Such a body of teachings centering on life and health integrates levels of body-mind-spirit.

In our time, we live in a natural and human world sorely in need of healing. We seek resources to heal the separations, the stuck points and the starvations of our world. Healing calls for respect and reciprocity.

We heal the new with insight from the old; we heal the old with insights from the new. Our commitment is to respect both East and West, both old and new, both outer and inner work. In this spirit, I wish to enter a caution of sorts.

In the Ch'an (or Zen) Buddhist tradition, it is said that *at the beginning of the journey*, a tree is a tree, a lake is a lake and a mountain is

---

THE WAY OF LAO TZU	THE WAY OF K'UNG TZU

INSIGHT
on how to get beyond
the "Law" of Aggression or "Tit for Tat" Action-Reaction

Return to one's original nature (*pu*)	Seek a common culture
Learn from nature's rhythms	Learn from the virtue of the ancients
Practice *Wei Wu Wei* = acting without producing adverse reaction	Act as *Chün-tzu* — the noble or superior-minded person Not as *Hsiao-jen* — the non-noble, small-minded person

NATURE OF THE PATH

This implies a Path of DIS-IDENTIFICATION	This implies a Path of RE-IDENTIFICATION
a process of simplification (radical letting go)	an awakening of aspiration (becoming large-minded)
Giving up desires and giving up concern for the views of others (becoming like a fool)	Giving to others the example of humane conduct (Goodness shaped by ritual/ceremony)

REALITY GROUNDING

The anchor of this way lies in NATURE	The anchor of this way lies in the FIVE RELATIONSHIPS
in the energy manifest, for example, in the Martial Arts or in Acupuncture	especially the central social virtues of Filial Piety and Fraternal Regard

KEY DISCIPLE

Chuang Tzu	Meng Tzu

---

a mountain; *in the midst of the journey*, a tree, a lake and a mountain are no longer what they appear to be; *at the end of the journey*, a tree is a tree, a lake is a lake, a mountain is a mountain.

In similar fashion, our comparative method is a process:

At the beginning, classic Chinese thinking will be used to highlight *differences* with the modern West. (Almost inevitably, we will tend to turn "different" into "better.")

In the midst of our journey, we may recognize how easy it is to fall into an *idolatry* of the ancient "superior" East over the modern, "benighted" West. Suddenly we realize that we are in a new version of the familiar ("us" vs. "them") trap, that we are now, in Frederick Franck's words, "playing 'I am Zennier than thou.' "

At completion, we make a breakthrough; we go beyond this new dualism. The deeper *commitment* is to both East and West, both Old and New, both Inner and Outer. Circling the globe from West to East will eventually bring us home. And yet we return with new eyes. We become, in a way, bi-ocular, seeing with both eyes more than one time and tradition. We become, in a modest way, bilingual, having more than one way to speak about life and living.

In fact, we go through the triad many times. At the start, to mark differences, we speak in the language of *either-or*, often setting a valid insight in too restrictive a container. In the midst of our efforts, we find ourselves favoring one thing at the expense of another and it dawns on us that we are in dualism still. At a provisional completion, we move to a deeper standpoint, one which can appreciate *both* how things stand at the surface *and* how they are at base.

Such is the rhythm of our exploration. Moreover, the purpose of our exploration is a practical one: *commitment to healing service*. Both Lao Tzu and Confucius forward this practical intent, with a view toward health and wholeness. For the ancients, wisdom is validated in life, and life is enriched by wisdom. For myself, I came to Eastern thought as did many others — in the sixties — when so much of life was coming apart. I came to Eastern thought with a practical intent and first encountered such thinking *as a living presence* through the artist Frederick Franck and his wife Claske. I grappled with Chinese philosophy (especially Taoist) in relationship with old friends who had become acupuncturists and who had, later, set up an institute to teach traditional Chinese acupuncture.[5] From friends who were also healers I saw explicitly the healing aspects of applied Chinese thought. I collaborated with these friends to design a program offering the healing principles of acupuncture to those in many walks of life. In this, I came more and more to add Confucian to Taoist insights in my own teaching and living.[6] Finally, with a nudge from the work of Thomas Berry, many things that I had been long pondering fell into place as what I now call the Seven Domains. In Part Two of this book, I describe the cycles of energy that underlie traditional Chinese medicine. In Part Three, I present the spheres of application, the seven domains in which we live. Throughout, I write to encourage healing service.

Having considered East and West, Old and New, Outer Kingliness and Inner Sageliness, we are now in a position to take an overview of this entire book, to see how *method* will be brought to bear on *content* for the sake of *healing service*. The next chapter is meant to display a map of the territory and to orient us for a journey through it.

Notes

[1] This is an ancient Chinese saying which marks well the relationship between the two strands of classical Chinese culture.

[2] See Thomas Berry, *Riverdale Papers on China*, privately printed, available from the author through the Riverdale Center, 5801 Palisade Avenue, Riverdale, New York 10471.

[3] For more on the historical background, see Charles O. Hucker, *China to 1850: A Short History* (Stanford., CA: Stanford University Press, 1978). Also note Herrlee G. Creel, *Chinese Thought: From Confucius to Mao Tse-Tung* (Chicago: University of Chicago Press, 1953).

[4] See Bruce Holbrook, *The Stone Monkey: An Alternative, Chinese-Scientific, Reality* (New York: William Morrow and Company, 1981).

[5] I identify these friends in the last section of the Acknowledgments.

[6] See Acknowledgments, footnote 1 and elsewhere in that introductory chapter for more on the SOPHIA project of the Traditional Acupuncture Institute.

CHAPTER THREE

FOURFOLD STRUCTURE: THE SQUARE WITHIN THE CIRCLE

"Nothing is wiser than the circle."

— Rilke[1]

The poet Rilke tells this story about God. In an early time, when people prayed with arms extended, God loved to reside in the warm, dark, mysterious human heart. Then, as time passed, people began to pray with hands folded like church steeples. God saw all the tall civic towers, castles with battlements and churches with great steeples pointed upward like armaments. They frightened God who retreated ever further into space. But the earth is round and one day, God noticed that the round earth was dark and fertile and mysterious — so like the welcoming human heart of old. So God entered into the heart of the earth and became one with the earth. One day, Rilke says, perhaps as we too notice the earth, while digging to the depth, we shall again find the mystery, which is also the source. "There is nothing wiser than the circle," says Rilke.[2]

A. THE SQUARE WITHIN THE CIRCLE

Recall the fantasy of an astronaut standing on the moon and looking back at earth through an ancient Chinese coin — the round coin, the square hole in the center, earth seen through this frame.

This book, like the square within the circle, has a fourfold arrangement:

       I.   Life as Ongoing Exploration
      II.   Life as Energy
     III. Life as Dwelling
     IV. Life as Healing Service

What was said earlier about this structure bears repeating. Just as the old Chinese coin represents earth as a square within the circle of the heavens, so our fourfold structure exists within a circle and creates a circular motion: making us aware that exploring life — as energy and as dwelling — is for the sake of healing service; making us aware that healing service to life — as dwelling and energy — requires ongoing exploration. All this is carried out under the image of the earth seen as a whole, in the service of life as it unfolds in space and time between the heavens and the earth.

The figure below shows us that the exploration is directed to the cycles of energy and the domains of dwelling, and the healing service is also directed to the cycles of energy and the domains of dwelling.

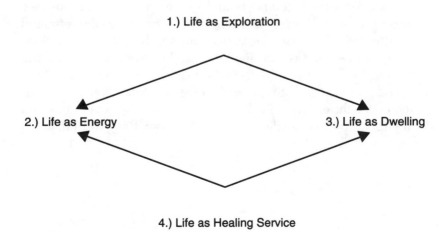

1.) Life as Exploration

2.) Life as Energy   3.) Life as Dwelling

4.) Life as Healing Service

A second mode of representation emphasizes the circular process

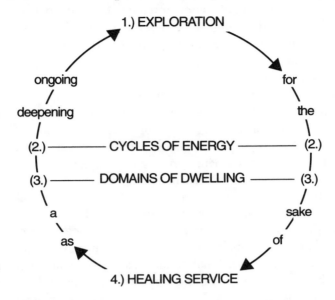

A third illustration represents the energy as an unfolding yin-yang circle and the domains for dwelling as five concentric rings between a mysterious center and an equally mysterious circumference:

In a circle, everything is and must be present from the beginning. Consider the movement of a circular dance. Is not every place on the circle beginning and ending? Does not every dancer lead and follow? On paper, we might describe the movements and countermovements of the dance sequentially; in the dance, they occur simultaneously; in the dance, they arise together.

In like manner, all is present in the principles of exploration. All is present in the unfolding cycles of energy. All is present in the spatio-temporal domains for dwelling. All is present in the image of healing service. However, on paper, in a book, I must proceed sequentially. I begin with a type of knowing, an ongoing exploration. However, ongoing exploration is for the sake of healing service, and what is said at the end about healing also belongs at the beginning to establish the conditions of listening. Ongoing exploration and healing service are partners. Furthermore, to understand healing service requires that we identify balances and imbalances in the cycles of energy. To understand who the patient is — individual, family, institution, culture, planet — requires that we identify the various contexts or domains of living. So we are caught by the circle itself. We must enter the circle somewhere and join the dance. I enter under the heading of Life as Exploration.

B. LIFE AS EXPLORATION: A REVIEW OF METHOD

Thus far in Part One, I have introduced a method of thinking that moves from West to East and back; from the new to the old and back; from outer kingliness to inner sageliness and back. In other words, the method is cross-cultural, cross-epochal, and transpersonal. Further-more, the exploration has a practical, healing intent. I can now add that the exploration will focus on *cycles of energy* (whose time is archetypal and recurring) and on *domains for dwelling* (whose time is novel and non-repeating). Lastly, since the exploration is for the sake of healing service, a certain attitude is needed toward the work as a whole. Lao Tzu would counsel us to approach our task in the manner of the ancient masters, to be:

> Watchful, like people crossing a winter stream.
> Alert, like those aware of danger.
> Courteous, like visiting guests.
> Yielding, like ice about to melt.
> Simple, like uncarved blocks of wood.

Hollow, like caves.
Opaque, like muddy pools.[3]

Confucius would recommend that we approach the work with the large-minded attitude of the noble person in us (*chün tzu*), rather than the small-minded attitude of the superficial person in us (*hsiao jen*).

C. LIFE AS ENERGY: THE WORLD IN CYCLIC MOTION

Life as energy can be viewed as a circle under two aspects. First, the energy moves cyclically — round and round. Second, the circle itself arises from a center, expands and returns to a center, much as certain flowers unfold in the morning and close inwardly in the evening.

First, consider the energy of life as cyclic movement. The energy (called chi) is often compared to breathing. Such "breathing" can be seen in nature. Think of a lake set between the heavens above and the earth beneath. The water cycle is then a visible "breathing between" the heavens and earth. Moisture evaporates and rises to form clouds; clouds open to rain. A life-sustaining, life-renewing cycle.

Graphically, we represent the cycle as a circle of rising and falling energy.

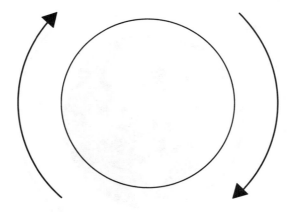

Draw such a circle on the sand. Start near your body and notice the movement: outward, away from you and then inward, back toward you — a movement of journeying afar and returning home. Here again we see the analogy with breathing — exhaling and inhaling. The exhaling is sometimes called the Outward Arc; the inhaling is sometimes called the Inward Arc.[4]

But there is something else. The circle of life as energy not only represents the movement of energy, the circle also has unfolding levels of differentiation, somewhat like a flower that unfolds from bud to leaves to blossom, somewhat like a flower that opens in the morning and closes in the evening. A flower that opens and closes represents another type of movement, a movement from the one to the many and then back from the many to the one.

In the ancient healing tradition, the outward unfolding proceeds in the following steps:

First, there is the Tao — Great Pattern of Life — which is unseen and unimagined, an empty space before anything is drawn.

Next, we see the Tao as manifest, imaged as a circle. The circle stands for the One. But as soon as the circle is drawn, twoness appears — up and down, front and back, left and right, inner and outer. Yin and yang.

Yin and yang reach harmony in the tai chi symbol.[5] *The tai chi symbol shall be our emblem for life as energy*. It reminds us of the energy as cyclic movement; it possesses the primary differentiation of the one into two. Yang energy is light, clear, upward and outward; yin energy is dark, mysterious, downward and inward.

The tai chi symbol — of the two joined in harmony — is like the bud of a flower. Next the flower unfolds to five petals: the five elements, the five seasons as shown below:

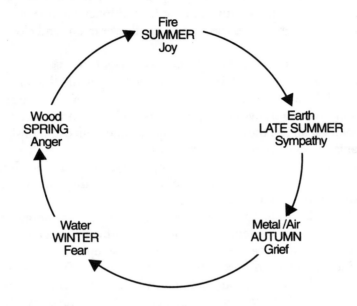

The next expansion moves from the five elements to the twelve officials. Energy is now differentiated into functions, as if on each petal of the flower further markings could now be seen.

We can imagine that this unfolding continues until the flower represents the three hundred and sixty points of a circle, until these very points are seen as reflecting everything in the visible universe — what the Taoists call The Ten Thousand Things. Thus, we come to think of the world as a flower, of the World Flower, a great lotus arising out of the still waters, opening and closing.

The differentiation, the breathing out, takes us from the one to the many. The reintegration, the breathing in, takes us from the many to the one. Parallel to the movement toward complexity as the flower unfolds, there is a movement of simplification inward, as the flower begins to close. In the inward movement, the Ten Thousand Things and the three hundred and sixty points simplify back into the twelve functions. The twelve disappear into the five elements. The five elements fade into the movement of yin and yang. Only the circle itself remains. Then it too returns into the mystery unseen.

Such is the world as cyclic energy — constantly moving as from season to season, constantly opening to multiplicity and returning to unity. The energy circles the flower; the flower opens and closes.

D. Life as Dwelling: The World as Seven Domains

Consider again a lake. Imagine a stone thrown into the mirror-like surface of the water. Watch the water ripple out in concentric circles — a mysterious center, five concentric rings, and a mysterious enveloping horizon. I shall call these circles "domains" and shall distinguish seven domains — seven concentric circles.

The seven domains are spatio-temporal contexts in which humans (and others) can consciously dwell.[6] As such, they are particular subpatterns of a total pattern.

The circles of energy appear in every domain. Life as energy stresses cyclic time — the ancient and archetypal rhythms, the recurring, the similar — like the steady time signature of a symphony. The domains introduce something different, like the symphony itself with themes and variations. The domains are defined by timespans, which allows the new, the surprising, the non-repeating, the unique. Life is lived in both the repeating rhythms and the surprising songs of each domain. The domains, however, sketch the songs, the narratives, the stories that occur in a set of nested timespans, namely: the moment, the lifetime, generational time, institutional time, the cultural time of the human race and the planetary time of the earth and all its inhabitants.

Think again of the concentric rings. Each context between the first circle (the center) and the seventh circle (the outer circumference) is a pattern within a pattern — nested contexts for dwelling. Each of these domains exhibits signs of health and illness, balance and imbalance. Each has the potential to be healer and to be patient.

The *first domain* — the innermost circle — is the bodily self where inner work is done. The self is like the point, a unique focus of activity. The self is also like a mirror, reflecting all the other circles. *The time of the first domain is the time of the moment.*

The *second domain* — the circle of two — focuses primarily on one-to-one relationships between persons. Friendship is the model here — friendship between two persons sufficiently grown to realize that each

---

stands in the midst of a lifetime — between a personal past and a still-to-be future. *The time of the second domain is the time of the lifetime.*

The *third domain* is the circle of three — of the three generations that define *a family over time.* In this domain, we stand within our generation, between the generation of our parents and the generation of our children. It is in this domain that we learn to honor our ancestors and to benefit our children. *The time of (at least) three generations is central to this third domain.*

The *fourth domain* is the circle of four — the "big four" institutions — economic and political, educational and religious — which interweave to create a social reality beyond the family. In ancient times, the fourth domain was composed of states within the kingdom; today, we speak more naturally of the institutional network within a nation. The "big four" institutions are, of course, a simplification of the institutional world. But they serve adequately to introduce the ordered network of rules, roles, and routines, of policies, procedures and power, that structure a world larger than family. Unlike most families, these institutions enter historical time. Specifically, they inhabit the time of the nation or, more accurately, the time of a particular historical epoch. *Centuries are the unit of time for the institutional network.*

The *fifth domain* — the fifth circle — is the cultural domain. The cultural domain gives to all within its sphere a particular color, taste, texture. This circle is shaped by myth and ritual, story and symbol, collective meaning and value. What unites diverse cultures is to see them against the background of the human story, the story of the human race. Cultural time may be spoken of in *epochs* that exist like chapters in the history of the species.

In this fifth domain, I will follow Thomas Berry in introducing five cultural epochs in the human story:[7] (i) a paleolithic, matricentric epoch, (ii) a tribal village epoch (stretching from neolithic times onward), (iii) a classical-traditional epoch, which gives rise to the great religions and philosophies, East and West, (iv) a scientific-technological epoch, and (v) an emerging ecological epoch.

The human story expands our sense of time from centuries to thousand-year units (millennia). The time scale of the human race reaches to a million or more years. Yet it will pale beside the earth's story and the story of the universe which is its background.

The *sixth domain* expands the circle to include the earth and all its inhabitants as a total environment. The sixth circle is earth itself seen as a self-sustaining, creative process.[8] To grasp this context is to go *beyond a human-centered view* (now called speciesism or anthropocentrism) *to a biocentric view,* which includes all living species and indeed their unique bioregions. *The history of earth itself takes us from epochs to aeons (thousands of millions of years). The earth is about 4.5 billion years old; earth's story is itself backgrounded by some 15 billion years of cosmic history.*

The *seventh domain* is the domain of mystery — a domain that is both timeless and within all time. Strictly speaking, the seventh domain is not a visible circle at all. It is more like the paper upon which we write, the canvas on which we draw, than the marking thereon.[9]

As mentioned, these seven domains are contexts in which we live.[10] They are nested contexts — like concentric circles. We inhabit all of the domains already and always, although in Part Three, we shall visit them one by one. The following chart may be a useful way of grasping (in preview fashion) the seven domains:

**THE SEVEN DOMAINS —
SEVEN CONTEXTS WITH ASSOCIATED TIME FRAMES**

1) THE PERSONAL DOMAIN —
THE TIME OF THE MOMENT
From the "now" of the child through the "now" of dispersed emotions to the "now" of the sage — the sphere of "inner work."

2) THE (1-TO-1) RELATIONAL DOMAIN —
THE TIME OF THE LIFETIME
Here we see the dynamics of pairs, of interactions across a range from enemy to stranger to neighbor to friend to beloved.

Round about adolescence, we begin to have a sense of our lifetime. Our past becomes problematic; our future, uncertain. So it is with others also. With this new sense of time and identity, we have a greater capacity both for manipulation and for friendship.

3) THE (THREE GENERATIONAL) FAMILY DOMAIN —
THE TIME OF GENERATIONS
When we have children (or accept responsibility for "the children"), the time of generations opens up for us. We come to think of our

---

generation, our parents' generation, and our children's generation. We see how the gifts and wounds of family history arise.

4) THE INSTITUTIONAL (OR KINGDOM) DOMAIN —
THE TIME OF THE NATION
(or, better, of the EPOCH in which the nation exists)
Particular INSTITUTIONS (e.g. governmental and economic, religious and educational) are part of a SYSTEM OF INSTITUTIONS. This interlocking system presently constitutes the nation state.

5) THE CULTURAL/HISTORICAL DOMAIN —
THE TIME OF THE HUMAN RACE
Culture is seen as that set of meanings, values, purposes, myths and rituals that establish the common sense of reality for a people. Today, we think of the *nation* as the prime carrier of culture (and we recognize sub-cultures within the nation). We acknowledge national culture as the foreground; we emphasize the *history of the race* as background. In particular, we find useful Thomas Berry's notion of five cultural epochs: the paleolithic, the neolithic-tribal, the classical, the technological, and the new emerging ecological epoch.

6) THE PLANET EARTH DOMAIN —
THE TIME OF COSMIC UNFOLDING
This is a domain where the human is situated in *the more than human* — where we come to realize our kinship with the animals, plants and elements of our shared earth. Also, we are coming to see the earth as a self-organizing, self-developing organism. Earth's story is embedded in the cosmic story. Consider these six cosmic periods (modified from Berry): (i) from the Fireball to the elements and galaxies, (ii) from the Milky Way to our solar system, (iii) earth in its physical formation, (iv) the emergence of plant life, (v) the emergence of (conscious) animal life, and (vi) the formation of the human and the development of the cultural epochs.

7) THE DOMAIN OF MYSTERY —
WITHIN AND BEYOND TIME
The circle whose center is everywhere; whose circumference, nowhere.

E. LIFE AS HEALING SERVICE

Using the method of exploration outlined in this introductory Part One, we will go on to examine life as energy and life as domains for dwelling in parts Two and Three. Part Four — Life as Healing Service — will complete the circle.

Recall that our exploration is, from the beginning, for the sake of healing service — a healing service attuned to the archetypal rhythms of cyclic life and the unique and unrepeatable timespans that mark the domains of life. The aim of the work remains constant: *to come to life more fully so as to serve life more wisely and more nobly* — in each of the domains of life, throughout each of the seasons of life.

Part Four draws together the lessons learned, and, in the process, returns us to the beginning again. Each time the cyclic energies and the temporal theatres of action are joined by healing awareness, we have completed one round of the circle. We return enriched to begin again, to continue life in deeper, more reflective, more creative ways. From ancient times, Lao Tzu reminds us that "returning is the movement of the Tao."[11] From our own time, the oft-quoted words of T.S. Eliot re-echo:

> We shall not cease from exploration
> And the end of all our exploring
> Will be to arrive where we started
> And know the place for the first time.[12]

Notes

[1] See Rainer Maria Rilke, trans. M.D. Herter Norton, *Stories of God* (New York: W.W. Norton & Company, 1963), "A Tale of Death and a Strange Postscript Thereto," pp. 87-96.

[2] *Ibid.*

[3] Lao Tzu, trans. Gia-Fu Feng and Jane English, *Tao Te Ching* (New York: Random House, 1972), chapter fifteen. Modified for inclusive language.

[4] See Frances Vaughan, *The Inward Arc: Healing and Wholeness in Psychotherapy and Spirituality* (Boston: Shambhala Press, 1986). Note also Ken Wilber, *The Atman Project*.

⁵ In chapter four, we shall see that yin and yang in harmony, by nature, give rise to the Creative Third.

⁶ Domains as spatio-temporal contexts are not *modes of thinking*. More specifically, the domains should **not** be viewed as *stages of thought*, in a Piaget-Kohlberg sense. First, as I have noted, the domains are not modes of thought. Second, one need not move through them in any invariant sequence. Third, the domains are not in hierarchical order in the sense that later or higher is better. For a fuller examination of Piaget-Kohlberg stage theory, see my "Kohlberg's Progress Toward Understanding the Moral Life" (unpublished Ph.D. thesis, University of North Carolina at Chapel Hill, 1982; available University Microfilms, Ann Arbor, Michigan).

⁷ See Thomas Berry, *The Dream of the Earth*, p. 93.

⁸ See *ibid.* See also J. E. Lovelock, *Gaia.*

⁹ See Ken Wilber's work for a parallel use of the background analogy, though Wilber uses this in relation to a mode of consciousness, and my domains are not defined as modes of consciousness. Note, for example, Ken Wilber, *The Atman Project*, as well as his *No Boundary: Eastern and Western Approaches to Personal Growth* (Boulder, CO: Shambhala Press, 1981).

¹⁰ There is nothing absolute in presenting the domains as seven. One could, no doubt, distinguish more domains — for example, particular institutions and the network of institutions, particular cultures within an epoch in the history of the human race, bioregions and their interrelationship to form the earth, and again, history of the planet and of the universe. Seven is manageable and gives sufficient scope to integrate insights from the Western social sciences and from the Chinese classics. Its scale is close to that of *The Great Learning*.

¹¹ See *Tao Te Ching*, chapter forty.

¹² T. S. Eliot, end of "Little Gidding" section of the *Four Quartets*, in *The Complete Poems and Plays: 1909-1950* (New York: Harcourt, Brace and Company, 1952), p. 145.

LIFE AS ENERGY

The World in Cyclic Motion

THE IMAGE:
THE BOAT ON THE LAKE

The man and the woman arise at sunrise in their cottage by the shore of the wide lake. The lake is a hidden place, surrounded by gentle mountains. The man and the woman gaze out at the early morning mists over the shimmering surface of the waters. After eating lightly, they take their small boat some distance from shore. All day they spend fishing on the deep lake. Mostly, they fish in silence; occasionally, they exchange a word, a look, a smile; always they feel themselves cradled by the water, between the spacious sky above and the steady earth beneath them. When evening approaches, they return to their cottage and eat some of what they have caught. How long has it been like this for them? How long have they known the cycles of day and night and of the turning of the seasons, here beside this lake? Night comes and the moon rises over the lake. The man and the woman watch the reflection — the moon on the waters — an invitation to the depth of dreams.

Part Two of this work explores the ancient cyclic rhythm of life — the cycle of yin-yang, of the five elements or seasons, of the twelve officials or functions. It is one and the same cycle — understood in terms of two aspects, then in terms of five phases, then in terms of twelve functions.

CHAPTER FOUR

THE ONE, THE TWO, AND THE THREE

Tao gave birth to One;
One gave birth to Two;
Two gave birth to Three;
Three gave birth to
the ten thousand things.

— *Lao Tzu*, The Tao Te Ching[1]

When the man and the woman were in their boat on the lake, they felt themselves surrounded by Nature. Figures in a boat on a lake in the midst of mountains — such is a familiar theme in Chinese landscape painting. The name for such painting is "shan shui" which means mountain and water. In such landscape painting, what is unsaid is as significant as what is said; empty space is as important as the forms that arise in and out of the space.

> Something mysteriously formed,
> Born before heaven and earth.
> In the silence and the void,
> Standing alone and unchanging,
> Ever present and in motion.
> Perhaps it is the mother of the ten thousand things.
> I do not know its name.
> Call it Tao.
> For lack of a better word, I call it great.
>
> Being great, it flows.
> It flows far away.
> Having gone far, it returns.[2]

When the man and the woman looked out in early morning from their cottage by the lake, they saw mist upon the water. The mist is an image of a breathing between the heavens and the earth — water evaporating to become clouds and to return as life-renewing rain. The all-pervasive energy that the Chinese call *chi* is likened to a breathing between heaven and earth, likened to steam vibrating the lid of a cooking pot of rice, likened to mist in the void from which all appear and to which all return.

On this view, *all things of form and name* are condensations of the void, configurations of the chi, fleeting patterns within the Great Pattern. Perhaps these patterns-thought-of-as-things are more like songs. The poet, Gary Snyder, notes that the Japanese term for song, *bushi* or *fushi*, means a whorl in the grain of wood, like a knot in a board. In Snyder's words, "It's an intensification of the flow at a certain point that creates a turbulence of its own which . . . sends out an energy of its own, but then the flow continues again."[3] Any object can be thought of as a sort of vortex, an intensification of energy within a larger pattern of energy. In this way, the mist is a manifestation of an unseen breathing, a sign of the larger cosmic pattern becoming partially visible at this place and time.

A. THE ONE BECOMES THE TWO

The circle is an image of the One — the Tao — as manifest.[4] A circle drawn with one brushstroke is a circle not perfectly round, nor perfectly closed — a human representation of wholeness. Such a circle has long symbolized a harmony and oneness that transcends dualism. Yet the moment the circle is drawn, a duality — not yet dualism, but a duality — appears. For once the circle is drawn, there is up and down, in and out, right and left, front and back, foreground and background. The world of form is a world wherein distinctions are made. Pairs of opposites are primary distinctions. The One gives birth to the Two — to distinctions, to opposites. Such is the nature of things.

Everywhere people have noticed opposites, how they dance together and how they become separate and alone. When the two aspects of things dance together, I shall call them *a complementary or harmonious two* and speak of *polarity* or *duality*. When the two aspects are seen as two separate "things," I shall call them *the disconnected or antagonistic two* and speak of *dualism*.

Yin and yang are the appropriate names for the aspects of complementary two. Yin and yang — in their harmonious interplay — are represented by the tai chi symbol.

Upward
and
Outward

Yang
Aspect

Downward
and
Inward

Yin
Aspect

Thus, the circle as wholeness becomes the circle dance of yin and yang in harmony and balance.

There is a mystery here — a mystery in three acts or three "moments." In the first "moment," a circle is drawn; unity is presented; and immediately polarity appears — foreground/background, inner/outer, etc. In this first moment, polarity or duality (unity and diversity, movement and constancy) are still connected in prior unity to the source. Such polarity or duality is benign; it arrives at the same instant that anything becomes manifest.

In the second "moment," however, we reflective humans arrive on stage. Now there is a new ingredient. We can affirm the motion and wholeness of life or remain in ignorance and blindness. In ignorance, what is whole is made partial; we experience *separation*. In ignorance, what is in motion (deeper than movement vs. rest) is forgotten; we experience *stuckness*. In ignorance, what is sufficient is seen as scarce; we experience various sorts of *starvation*. Such ignorance brings on the Defect, causes the Fall, lulls us to sleep.

Nonetheless, a third "moment" is possible — a moment when we reclaim unity and diversity, movement and constancy, fullness and emptiness. Then yin and yang are again seen as arising out of unity and remaining in unity's embrace. Separateness, stuckness and starvation are "seen and seen through." Yin and yang again dance together.[5]

Where this mutual arising is never lost or where, after being temporarily lost sight of, is regained, we speak of the Creative Third.[6] The Creative Third — represented by the tai chi symbol — is a space of possibility beyond dualism, a freeing of the heart for loving service. In the Creative Third, we embrace unity and diversity from a standpoint of deeper union. What was thought to be separate is seen from a deeper space — a space where surface separation and connection are in a dance.[7] What was thought to be stuck is seen from a deeper place — a place where surface rest and movement are part of a more fundamental motion of life itself. What was thought to be insufficient is seen from a deeper standpoint — a standpoint where surface having and not having is compatible with a deeper sense that, in truth, we have all we need to be human.

B. Yin-Yang as Aspects, Phases and Sufficiencies

In the prologue scene, the man and the woman were together through a day from sunrise and morning to moonrise and night. The basic cycle of yin and yang is well seen in terms of night and day. Here yang is the energy of the day, of the sky, of the sun; yin is the energy of the night, of the earth, of the moon. Yin and yang are distinct, but not separate. Even in the night, there is a touch of yang as light is reflected from the moon; even in the day, there is a touch of yin in the shadows and the shade by the shore of the lake. Light and darkness arise together as two aspects of the same phenomenon, distinct but not separate.

The rising energy is from midnight to midday; the falling energy is from midday to midnight. Yin energy and yang energy are two movements of the one rotation of Earth. Day is seen as the time for activity; night is seen as the time for rest. Activity and rest arise together. In like fashion, initiation and completion, speaking and listening, giving and receiving — all are two phases of one motion. Yin and yang remind us that day and night — movement and rest — are phases in a deeper motion of life.

The man and woman lived beside a lake surrounded by mountains. Consider one of these mountains. In the morning, we can identify the sunny side and the shady side of this one mountain. The Chinese characters for yin and yang come from this image. In its core meaning, yang refers to "the sunny side of the mountain," while yin refers to "the shady side of the mountain." One mountain; two aspects. Furthermore, sunny and shady are relative and contextual. What is the sunny side in the morning can become the shady side in the afternoon.

Yin and yang stress the interconnection of life. "Sunny" and "shady" are distinct, but not separate, aspects of one mountain. Sunrise and sunset are continuous phases of one motion, distinguishable but not stuck. Warmth and coolness together provide us with what we need. Interconnected life arises from sufficiency, not scarcity. Yin and yang remind us that life is sufficient, that starvation need not be, that what is needed is close at hand.

Together, yin and yang — represented by the tai chi (Creative Third) symbol — remind us that life at its core takes us beyond the Separated, the Stuck, and the Starved. The imbalance labeled "starvation" is better examined in the next chapter. But separation and stuckness can be seen even in the compass of the two — the context of this chapter on yin and yang.

C. ANTAGONISTIC OPPOSITES: THE RISE OF THE SEPARATED AND THE STUCK

Opposites, duality, twoness — this we took to be neutral, like the front and the back of one hand. Yin and yang dancing together achieve such a wondrous complementarity that we can hardly say who is leading and who is following. A dance is one reality. In the dance, there is motion and rest; there is distinctness and togetherness — all in one dance. In distinctness, the dancers may stand apart; in collaboration, they become a part of a larger pattern. They emerge and merge. Here the energies are distinct but not at war.[8]

How is it that we so easily slip from dualities into dualisms? First, instead of seeing two aspects of a single reality, we often regard the two aspects as *separate* and think of them as separate things. What belongs together spatially, we separate and "thingify." Second, instead of seeing two phases of one integral rhythm, we often become *stuck* — frozen in one phase of the movement. What belongs together dynamically, we paralyze and fixate. We may dislike one phase (the night, the winter) and like the other (the day, the summer). We may desire one and fear the other; value one and disvalue the other. In such fashion, we see *what is before us* as *separated* and *stuck*.

Consider two examples. The first example has to do with how I regard myself. In my body, in my self, I can experience separation from my deeper wholeness. Perhaps I like to receive but not to give, to take in but not let go. I may hoard possessions or power or prestige. Like

Dickens' Scrooge, I may become stuck in one part of a cycle and separated from my natural wholeness, separated from my ability to give as well as receive. Notice: I am *stuck* in the movement of my life and I am *separated* from the wholeness of my life. For I identify only with receiving and deny my capacity to give. I *partialize* myself—identifying with only a portion of my wholeness, becoming this but not that. I *paralyze* myself, becoming fixated in one moment of the cycle.

A second example concerns not a single person but how a couple regards its relationship. In the prologue story, the man and woman seemed bonded in a true marriage, a deep unity wherein real difference was respected. The couple may indeed be joined in such a marital reality, yet *we* may miss seeing their prior union. To us, the man and the woman may seem separate — two solitudes. We may see each as a separate "thing." If we do, we will next be tempted to assign yang qualities only to the man, and yin qualities only to the woman.

Suppose next that the couple comes to believe this is the way matters stand. If the man believes this, he will become stuck in only one half of the movement of life — the initiating, outward-looking aspect. He will tend to become separated from some parts of his nature and solely identified with others. If the woman believes this, she will become stuck in only one half of the movement of life — the receiving, inward-looking aspect. She will tend to become separated from some parts of her nature and solely identified with others. Both will become caricatures, fixed stereotypes. Each is then fated to have only one thing, to be only one thing. Sharing is impoverished. Giving and receiving cease to offer the richness available when they proceed from wholeness. The two are separated and stuck; the marriage is fractured and distorted.

To summarize, opposites that are separate and stuck come to be seen in either-or terms. Next, valuing enters and more opposition ensues. One pole of the detached opposites is labeled "good"; the other is labeled "bad." The stereotyped two are now cast into superior-inferior roles. What was healthy becomes dis-ease; what was in balance becomes cancerous; what was in the movement of life becomes deadened and disabled. The pair exhibits pathology.

When separation and stuckness occur in a person or pair, we are far from the tai chi symbol, far from authentic yin and yang. Yin and yang, by their nature, are connected, are two aspects of one underlying reality. Yin and yang, by their nature, are in phased, cyclic movement, like the beating of the heart, like the movement of the breath. Yin and yang, by their nature, are never extremes, rather they always present both sides of a sufficiency. This is shown in the tai chi symbol by the small circle of yin in the yang and the small circle of yang in the yin.

D. Coming to Life More Fully:
Reversing Separation and Stuckness

The American Plains Indians say that all beings know "the Give-away," except the human ones, who have to learn.[9] We must "give away" to overcome our separateness — give away our identifying with "this" but not "that," let go of our separateness, reclaim the deeper wholeness which we are. We must give away to overcome our stuckness — give away our wishing to be "here" but not "there," let go of our stuckness in rest or movement, reclaim the deeper motion which we are.[10]

Separateness occurs in either-or thinking. Psychologists influenced by Neuro-linguistic Programming (NLP) have a saying: "If you have one choice, you have no choice; if you have two choices, you are caught on the horns of a dilemma; only with three choices do you begin to be free."[11] The third is not simple compromise; the third opens a space of possibility beyond either-or.

Stuckness occurs when in thoughts and actions, we are in a rut, fixed by our attractions or aversions or both. We like the day and fear the night; we value upward energy and disvalue downward energy. We are not at home at all points in the cycle. Gestalt psychologist Frederick "Fritz" Perls speaks of "the stuck point" in therapy. He mentions several ways through the stuck point: grief, joy, anger and orgasm.[12] Zen masters in the Rinzai school intensify stuckness for the sake of break-through; Zen masters in the Soto school teach how barriers drop away like ripe fruit falling from the tree of their own accord. Stuckness can be transcended in many ways.

When we cease to feel separate, sharing can arise. When we cease to feel stuck, the *motion that is our lives* can be celebrated and whatever is appropriate (whether movement or stillness) can find a place.

The Creative Third arises whenever yin and yang dance together. The space of that dance *is* the Creative Third. We humans experience the Creative Third as a space of freedom, where the heart is touched, where truth is gentle and rich in possibility, where beauty seems abundant, where virtually anything is possible, where we become more our unique selves and more supported by the entire "pattern that connects."[13]

When we overcome separation and stuckness (even temporarily), we are in the place of possibility, of freedom, of the Creative Third. We feel joyously whole — uniquely ourselves and completely a part of the wider dance. This is the space of the inner marriage, the harmonious joining of the yin and yang within us. It brings to life also the outer marriages, the loving partnerships from which creative gifts spring.

Such is the message of coming to life more fully in the one circle, differentiated into the harmonious two, yin and yang. Throughout this chapter, we worked with fundamental contrast: the two. We mentioned *union undifferentiated* (the mysterious One). We noted *union differentiated but harmonious* (the manifest One which simultaneously gives rise to yin and yang). We explored *union apparently severed and motion apparently stopped* (the antagonistic two). Finally, we saw *union reclaimed*, where the harmonious two generate the space of possibility called the Creative Third.

Notes

1. *Tao Te Ching*, chapter forty-two, translation by Henry Wei.

2. Lao Tzu, *Tao Te Ching*, Gia-Fu Feng and Jane English translation, chapter twenty-five.

3. See Gary Snyder, "Knots in the Grain," in *The Real Work: Interviews & Talks 1964-1979* (New York: New Directions, 1980), p. 44. Snyder notes that this parallels what Black Elk says concerning the American Plains Indian view of physical nature.

4. Compare the eighth of the ten Oxherding Pictures. See Philip Kapleau, *The Three Pillars of Zen* (Boston: Beacon Press, 1967).

5. My account (developed in collaboration with my SOPHIA teaching partner, Julia Measures) differs from that of N. J. Girardot. For me, the one, the two and the three appear in the manifest world (as opposed to the Tao which is unmanifest and cannot be named); for Girardot, they are prior to the manifest world. See N.J. Girardot, *Myth and Meaning in Early Taoism: The Theme of Chaos (Hun-Tun)*, (Berkeley, CA: University of California Press, 1983).

6. On the Creative Third, see J. C. Cooper, *Yin and Yang: The Taoist Harmony of Opposites* (Wellinborough, Northamptonshire, England: Aquarian Press, 1981), chapter eight. Cooper uses the term "the Resolving Third."

7. In chapter one, I first suggested that the East prefers a surface-vs.-depth model. I shall return again to this theme in Part Four.

8   For another discussion on what makes "boundaries into battlelines," see Ken Wilber, *No Boundary*.

9   See Hyemeyohsts Storm, *Seven Arrows* (New York: Ballantine Books, 1972).

10   My notion of "the deeper motion which we are" echoes a similar notion in Robert Kegan's work. See Robert Kegan, *The Evolving Self: Problem and Process in Human Development* (Cambridge, MA: Harvard University Press, 1982), p.169 ("the evolutionary motion which we are") and p. 209 ("the motion of life itself"). See also pp. 81-82.

11   I heard this quote from NLP psychologist, Leslie Cameron-Bandler at a Lifeskills workshop in Winston-Salem, North Carolina, Mar. 15-16, 1986.

12   See Frederick Perls, *Gestalt Therapy Verbatim* (New York: Bantam, 1971), pp. 59-62. Also see Perls, *The Gestalt Approach & Eye Witness to Therapy* (New York: Bantam, 1976).

13   The phrase "the pattern that connects" is Gregory Bateson's. See Bateson, *Mind and Nature: A Necessary Unity* (New York: Bantam, 1980) and also his *Steps to an Ecology of Mind* (New York: Ballantine, 1972). I am using the phrase in a sense wider than Bateson does. For me, it is coextensive with the Tao.

CHAPTER FIVE

SEASONS OF LIFE: THE CYCLE OF THE FIVE ENERGIES

We are leaving our time now. We are leaving our time now.
Some places, time goes more slowly; some places, faster.
We are leaving our time now.
There are Four Directions: East, West, North, South.
We honor the Four Directions, and we also honor the
Fifth Direction: the vertical, which is in us, here tonight.

> — *The poet Robert Bly's mode of opening a "space and time*
> *for listening," before he tells a certain kind of story[1]*

Consider a single tree, standing empty of leaves and alone in the snow, austere against the winter sky. We are struck by the contrast, and sketch the tree using coal-black ink on bare white paper. A single contrast, black against white.

Think now of the same tree in the cycle of four seasons: winter giving way to spring and summer, summer giving way to autumn and winter. Here, we may wish to increase the colors available: to show greens and reds and yellows and blues as well as blacks and whites. More complexity, more colors used to express it.

In the previous chapter, we began with a circle differentiated into two halves; in this chapter, we mark the same circle with four directions, four seasons, four quarters. The circle is the same, and the same dynamics of harmony and disharmony affect the circle, whether seen in halves or seen in fourths. Separation, stuckness and starvation are possible whether the cycle is simple (day/night) or more complex (the four seasons).[2]

When harmony is present between the two halves, we speak of yin and yang; we draw the tai chi symbol in the center; we note the Creative Third, which expresses and effects the harmony of the two. When harmony is present among the four aspects, we can again draw the tai chi symbol in the center and note the fifth element, which expresses and effects a harmony of the four. Same tree, same circle. Now, one contrast; now, more than one contrast.[3]

A. THE FOUR DIRECTIONS

Let us move into the space of the four directions simply and slowly. In the illustration below, we see the world, as if facing south.

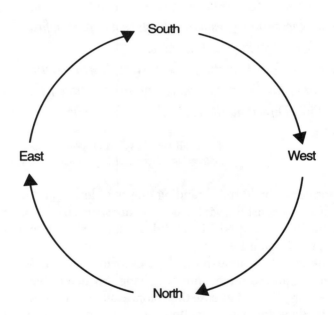

For those of us in the United States, Europe and China who live above the equator, the north reminds us of cold and the south reminds us of warmth. The cycle of the four directions — when put in motion

— easily turns into the clockwise movement of the four seasons:

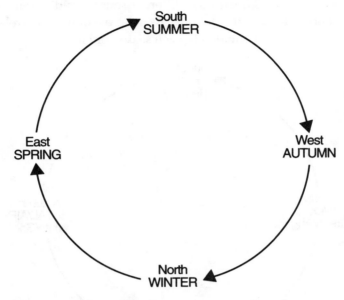

Each of these four seasons has a special quality of energy. Among the ancient Chinese, the quality of energy was expressed as an element or phase. The element or phase energies are exhibited below:

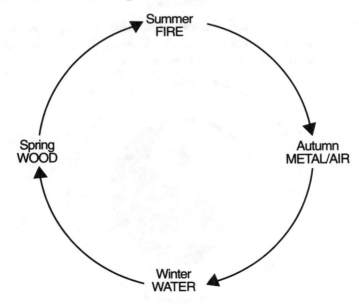

According to the ancient Chinese tradition, the energies come to be experienced (in accord with the different senses) as different colors, sounds, odors, tastes and emotions. As a sample of these correlations, let us add a color and emotion to each season or element.[4]

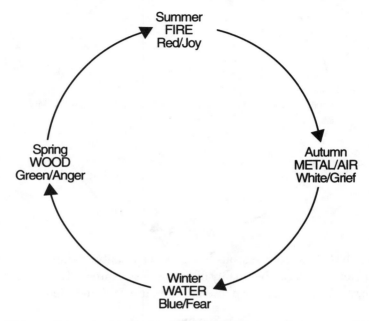

When all is going well, the four are distinct, *not separate*; the four are flowing one into another, *not stuck*. When this harmony prevails, the tai chi symbol may be placed in the center, thus:

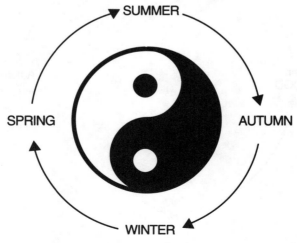

B. FIVE ELEMENTS AND FIVE SEASONS

Sometimes the fifth element or phase is placed in the center, where the tai chi symbol is above.[5] The fifth element expresses a harmonizing of the four, just as the Creative Third expresses a harmonizing of the two. How is the fifth element or phase represented? As the energy of earth — earth as one of the five aspects of the whole (not Earth as the planet itself). Earth as the energy of harvest, of nourishment, of connection.

1. Earth as an Element in the Center

When Earth is placed in the center, Earth as an energy joins the four and partakes somewhat of the nature of each. Here one may think of the transition times between the seasons, where a hint of all seasons can be sensed. Earth in the center suggests a Minister of Transport, to connect each to each and convey nourishing food needed by the whole. In the figure below, the earth as an energy with its colors and emotions is displayed in the center of the four:

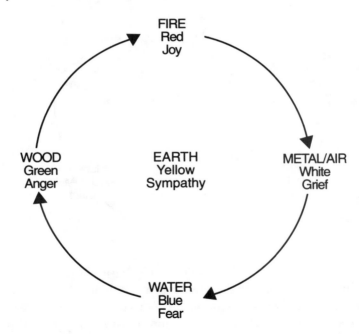

FIRE
Red
Joy

WOOD
Green
Anger

EARTH
Yellow
Sympathy

METAL/AIR
White
Grief

WATER
Blue
Fear

2. Earth on the Circle of the Five

The four elements with Earth in the center point up some truths about the whole; Earth can be seen as connecting the four. However, the *flow of energy* is not well displayed in this configuration. The remedy for this is an arrangement wherein earth as an element takes its place on the circle and is represented as a fifth season, late summer (what we sometimes call Indian summer). The season late summer is very much about harvest, about nourishment distributed. Late summer also conveys well the experience of a blend of all the other seasons, for, in late summer, a lingering taste of spring and summer blends with anticipations of autumn and winter. The arrangement of the five seasons is as follows:

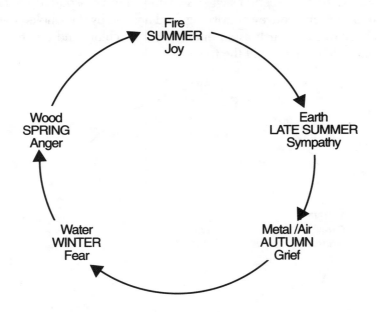

3. The Flow of Five Seasons

Think of the man and the woman living in their cottage by the lake. They have lived there for many years, seen the seasons change around their lake, experienced the same region transformed by the different energies in the cycle of a year. As we move from the two to the five, we move from a day and night to the larger circle of a year. With the expansion to five, we have more space to feel the energy move.

Let us begin in the depth of *winter*. Life is present but hidden as in the roots of trees, as in the deep waters. The waters are the place of beginnings, of birthing. To go into the waters is to surrender to a greater power, to face the not yet known, to move through fear to trust.

The seeds of new possibility grow in the greening energy of *spring*.[6] The force of growing life is formidable; vegetation sprouts forth, the trees renew their leaves. The energy of growth, when thwarted, is expressed in anger.

In *summer*, a full extension and maturity are felt. The sun brings abundant life and light and warmth. Abundance gives a sense of joy to be felt, expressed, shared.

Late summer reminds of earth's plenitude and marks the time for harvest. The gifts of spring and summer must now be gathered and used or stored for use. What is not taken up will rot and return to the earth. What is gathered up is meant to be given away, distributed, conveyed to all parts of the commonwealth so as to continue life.

Autumn comes with its chill. The air is crisp and clear. The leaves become brilliant before fading and dropping away. The energy is unmistakably moving downward and inward. The energy of Metal, of quality and respect and integrity, marks the season like the sound of a wondrous temple bell. Before one can be asked to let go, acknowledgment must be given. In the acknowledgment and the letting go is the quality of this season. Winter is again approaching — an ending and beginning.

4. The Seasons of a Life

When my daughter was little, she went to Montessori school. When a child had a birthday, part of the celebration was a ritual. Classmates and teachers would sit on the floor in a circle. A lighted candle would be placed in the center of the circle — a symbol of the sun. The lights would be turned out. The birthday child would carry a globe of the earth and circle the sun, once, twice, three times . . . up to the age the child was. One passage around the sun for each year of life. Such is the cyclic rhythm.

In reality, the earth carries us round the sun; in each passage, we experience the changing energies as seasons. But there are cycles within cycles. For we may see our life as a year and speak of the seasons of our life. Suppose we see the circle as a lifetime.[7] Perhaps we imagine it thus:

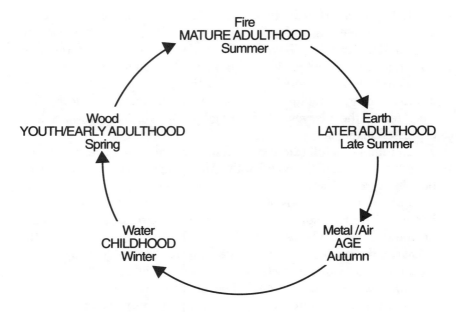

Fire
MATURE ADULTHOOD
Summer

Earth
LATER ADULTHOOD
Late Summer

Wood
YOUTH/EARLY ADULTHOOD
Spring

Metal /Air
AGE
Autumn

Water
CHILDHOOD
Winter

Furthermore, *within each period of life*, there is the cycle of five —
a beginning, a growth, a maturing, a harvesting, and a letting go.
Likewise, *within each year* within each period of life, we again find the
five. So also within the scope of a month or day or hour. In the smallest
exchange, there is beginning, growth, maturing, harvesting, and
letting go.

C. THREE OBSTACLES IN THE CIRCLE OF THE FIVE

Whether the one circle is seen as yin-yang or five elements, the same
chi energy is at work throughout, and the same dynamics repeat. Yin and
yang alternate in the rhythm of night and day, from midnight to midday.
The very same alternation is seen in the compass of a year — from
solstice to solstice. At the winter solstice, we find a turning point. The
days begin to lengthen; the energy rises into spring and summer. At the
summer solstice, we find a turning point. The days begin to shorten; the
energy recedes through late summer and autumn into winter. From
winter through spring to summer we have the upward, outward yang
half of the cycle. From late summer through autumn back into winter
we have the downward, inward yin half of the cycle. The two aspects —
yin and yang — remain present in the cycle of the five (and in each season
of a season).

What then prevents health and wholeness? What constricts our coming to life more fully?

In discussing yin and yang, I mentioned how we become *separated* and *stuck*. Now, in the same circle expanded to the five, we can recapulate and add a third feature: being *starved*.

The first obstacle is *being separated*. To become *separated* is to believe we are this and not that. In the circle of the five, we see more ways to become separated from the whole. We can develop a liking for only one elemental energy, defining ourselves as only that. For example, we can become our fear or anger. We can identify with sentimental "joy" or overprotective sympathy. We can become our grief. By fixating on one of the five, we both distort its meaning and think ourselves separated from the rest. Aversion to an element is another way to become separated from the elemental gifts.

The second obstacle is *being stuck*. To become *stuck* is to allow only some phases while resisting others. In the circle of the five, we can become stuck in one phase of the cycle. For example, we may become stuck in a particular season of life — stuck in beginnings and unable to grow; stuck in the energy of growth without prizing maturity; stuck in a version of maturity without moving to the harvest time of distributing one's gifts to another generation; stuck in mentoring and unable to enter the forest of the sage.

The third obstacle is *being starved*. To become *starved* is not to have what is needed in the appropriate amount, at the suitable time, in a fitting manner.[8] My sense of the term "starved" is thus wider than the ordinary meaning. Here, one can "starve" by overdoing and by underdoing, by having something good too early or too late, by being given the "right" thing in the wrong manner, etc.

We can be starved in our bodies, mind/hearts, and spirits. *At the level of our bodies, we can be starved for the gifts the Five Elements give.*

- The element *Water* quenches thirst, preserves the fluids of our bodies, encourages fluidity, and depth.
- The element *Wood* appears in plants that foster our growth, in trees that give shelter, in the ability to renew. The living tree is also a symbol of life itself, and a symbol of all who live between earth and sky. Like the tree, we are an intermediary reality, drawing nourishment from both the heavens and the earth,

needing both necessity and possibility, rooted in earth and growing toward the sky.[9]

- The element *Fire* gives light and warmth, in lamps and hearth.
- The element *Earth* gives us food and a homeplace.
- The element *Metal/Air* — most rarefied in air, most dense in diamonds — gives us breath itself, structure, character, gem-like quality.

But *starvation can also occur at the level of mind/heart*. We can look at emotional needs — how such needs can be blocked, how such needs can be met. Here, I acknowledge the work of a colleague, Fritz Frederick Smith, M.D., by using his correlation between the five energies as emotions and five healing tasks.[10]

- *Fear* is the emotion connected with the element Water. *Fear* calls us to renew *trust*. One can be starved for trust — in oneself, others, and as a basic trust in life. When caught up in fear, we need help to see what can be relied on. When a child is afraid in the night, parents seek to reassure that everything is all right. At the moment it is not, yet at some level it is. To rephrase an old adage: "Fear knocked. Trust answered. No one was there."
- *Anger* is the emotion connected with the element Wood. *Anger* calls us beyond the task of righting wrongs to a level of *forgiveness*, or basic *acceptance*, needed for growth. We can be eaten up with anger and starved for a type of forgiving acceptance that allows us to forgive ourselves, others, and the source of our trust. Here we touch on that most difficult saying: "To understand all is to forgive all."
- *Joy* is the emotion connected with the element Fire. *Joy* calls us to *companionship*. Joy is often caricatured as sentimentality, hollow optimism, forced "happiness," addictive pleasure. Often when we are starved for true joy, we are also starved for solid, honest friendship. True joy is inclusive of others. As it is said: "Sorrow shared is halved; joy shared is doubled."
- *Sympathy* is the emotion connected with the element Earth. *Sympathy* calls us, beyond condescension, to real *service*. Sympathy can be distorted into overprotectiveness and pity. When that is so, sympathy is still subtly centered on us. Genuine service does not diminish either the one serving or the one being served. We can be starved for the sort of sympathy that issues in service.

The Hindu deity Hanuman offers every act to Rama (God). Kneeling before Rama, he says: "When I know who I am, I *am* you. When I don't know who I am, I *serve* you."[11]

- *Grief* is the emotion connected with the element Metal/Air. *Grief* calls us to *surrender*. In Autumn, the leaves often go crimson and gold before letting go. So also we need deep acknowledgment before we can let go. We can be starved for such acknowledgment, starved by the inability to let go. No one need minimize the difficulties here. Such surrender takes us back into the unknown, into the fearful waters. Here, as elsewhere, we need the assistance of all the other gifts or tasks: trust, forgiveness, companionship and service. T. S. Eliot points to the price of surrender when he speaks of "a condition of complete simplicity (Costing not less than everything)."[12]

At the level of spirit, we can also experience a sense of being starved.[13] The spiritual dimension links us more deeply to all that is — ourselves, others, and our source. It calls us to the depth of life — to the deep waters — and situates us in the cosmic context. It encourages our growth with many spring-like renewals.

A central mark of the spiritual is discerning joy. Another mark is access to imagery, dreams and a sense of calling. The spiritual dimension likewise gives an ease with paradox, and an appreciation of the archetypal. Always, the wisdom eye sees compassionately, with gentle humor, the profound in the simple, the pattern in the particular. The spiritual is also expressive — connected with the artist within. The depths of life are expressed in art and poetry, story and myth, and in the deeds and gestures of ordinary and extraordinary people. Lastly, the spiritual holds the power to bring life to life, to actualize meaning and value, to unfold a life as service, and to acknowledge the sacred worth of all that is.

To feel one is cut off from the things of the spirit is to experience a kind of starvation. One seems cut off from connection, unaware of one's kinship with the Whole, out of touch with the depth of one's life. In the words of Seppo: "We are like those who, immersed in water, stretch out their hands begging for a drink."[14]

D. To Come to Life More Fully in the Circle of the Five

Three signs of imbalance are (1) being separated, (2) being stuck and (3) being starved. These imbalances are real and account for much of the sorrow of the world. To come to life more fully is to acknowledge and move beyond this condition of separation, stuckness and starvation. In truth, we are already deeply interrelated with *all that is*; we are already in the motion of the dance; we have, on this bounteous planet, all that is needed. Our task is, perhaps, to make visible what already lies present, to awaken hearts so that what is most true is what is most relied upon.

In many if not all contexts, something is not altogether missing; rather, in Dianne Connelly's phrase, it is "showing up as missing."[15] Yet, at least in the everyday world, a doubt can be heard. Is there not work to be done to feed the hungry, clothe the naked, shelter the homeless, comfort the sick and be present to the imprisoned? Are there not terrible lacks of food and shelter, education and employment, health care and housing? Are there not frightening signs of indignity and cruelty, discrimination and despair? Is there not something to "do," besides letting go?

Such issues are political as well as personal; as such, they cannot be adequately addressed until the domains of life are distinguished in Part Three. However, even at this juncture, there is a way of seeing the energy that reminds us of corporate work, a way that stresses *task* and *function*. This is the circle of the twelve, of the officials who tend the life of the kingdom. To this expansion, we now turn.

Notes

[1] Bly has several versions of this "cosmosizing of space and time." I first heard him use this device at a poetry reading done at Meredith College in Raleigh, NC, on April 8, 1988. That event was recorded by the Raleigh Men's Center, and tapes are available for purchase.

[2] Starvation as a type of imbalance is more easily seen in the circle of the four (or five) elements.

[3] For the ancient Chinese, odd numbers (such as 1, 3, 5) bespeak time and heaven-inspired harmony. Even numbers (such as 2, 4, 8) remind us of space and rootedness in earth. After a glimpse of the mysterious Creative Third, we return to earth with the four directions.

⁴ For more on the elements and their associations, see Dianne M. Connelly, *Traditional Acupuncture: The Law of the Five Elements*, (Columbia, MD: The Centre for Traditional Acupuncture, rev. ed. 1979). See also Elson M. Haas, *Staying Healthy with the Seasons* (Berkeley, CA: Celestial Arts, 1981).

⁵ See, for example, the late Taoist work, the *Hua Hu Ching* in *The Complete Works of Lao Tzu: Tao Teh Ching and Hua Hu Ching*, translation and elucidation by Taoist Master Ni, Hua-Ching (Los Angles, CA: College of Tao and Traditional Healing, 1989).

⁶ The theme of this greening power is evident in the 12th century mystic Hildegard of Bingen. She speaks of "veriditas." See *Illuminations of Hildegard of Bingen*, text by Hildegard of Bingen with commentary by Matthew Fox (Sante Fe, NM: Bear and Company, 1985).

⁷ I think of Freud's famous comment that maturity is the *ability to love* [sustain relationships of intimacy] and the *ability to work* [ability to persist in our tasks]. I think also of Erik Erikson's well-known stages of life. Late Summer correlates well with Erikson's period of generativity. See Erik H. Erikson, *Childhood and Society* (New York: Norton, 1950) and *Insight and Responsibility* (New York: Norton, 1964). On mentorship, see Laurent A. Daloz, *Effective Teaching and Mentoring* (San Francisco: Jossey-Bass, 1986).

⁸ My formulation here borrows from Aristotle on the virtuous [read healthy and balanced] person. See Aristotle, *The Nichomachean Ethics*, trans. Terence Irwin (Indianapolis, IN: Hackett Publishing, 1985).

⁹ On the need for both necessity and possibility, see Ernest Becker, *The Denial of Death* (New York: Free Press, 1973).

¹⁰ Fritz Smith is a fellow Board member of the Traditional Acupuncture Institute, the creator of Zero Balancing, and the author of *Inner Bridges: A Guide to Energy Movement and Body Structure* (Atlanta, GA: Humanics New Age, 1986).

¹¹ I take the story from Ram Dass and Paul Gorman, *How Can I Help?: Stories and Reflections on Service* (New York: Alfred Knopf, 1986), p. 226.

¹² See the end of the *Four Quartets, op. cit.* On surrender, see also Elisabeth Kubler-Ross' work on the stages of dying in her book, *On Death and Dying* (New York: Macmillan, 1970) as well as Elisabeth Kubler-Ross, ed., *Death: The Final Stage of Growth* (Englewood Cliffs, NJ: Prentice-Hall, 1975).

¹³ For some remarks on the spirits associated with the elements, see Claude Larre, Jean Schatz, and Elisabeth Rochat de la Vallee, *Survey of Traditional Chinese Medicine*, trans. S. E. Stang (Columbia, MD: Traditional Acupuncture Institute, 1986), esp. pp. 179-181 and 115-116. The spirits of the elements are somewhat elusive and often contrapunctual to other features of the elements; they call us strongly to the interrelation of the whole. I discuss

this level without explicit correlations to the elements, more by way of a speculation than an attempt at exegesis.

[14] Quoted in Frederick Franck, *The Book of Angelus Silesius* (New York: Random House, 1976), p. 58.

[15] See Dianne M. Connelly, *All Sickness is Homesickness* (Columbia, MD: Centre for Traditional Acupuncture, 1986).

CHAPTER SIX

THE KINGDOM OF THE TWELVE AND BEYOND

"The Kingdom is within."

— New Testament

The analogy is an old one: the image of the body; the image of the kingdom.[1] A parallel is presented between the kingdom as a structure or process of life and the body as a structure or process of life. To elaborate this analogy, we must draw upon a medical classic: *The Yellow Emperor's Classic of Internal Medicine (Huang Ti Nei Ching).*[2]

The bodily analogy is this: there are various energy systems at work within the body. Classical acupuncture distinguishes twelve basic pathways (meridians). These lines of circulation are mainly named for organs (e.g. heart, liver, lungs, kidneys). However, naming them thus has its dangers: it tends to make us think of things, not energy systems; it tends to make us picture organs in the Western sense rather than lines of circulation or functions in the service of life. In chapter eight of the *Nei Ching*, each of the twelve "organs" (or functions in service of life) is spoken of as an official with a charge. For example, the heart is lord and sovereign; the lungs are minister and chancellor; the liver is general of the forces to protect life, etc.

What is new here is a clearer sense of *function*. Each of these twelve subsystems (which arise out of the five elements) fulfill *functions* in the individual body-mind-spirit. When thought of as performing functions, the organs-meridians-pathways are spoken of as *officials* in a kingdom. To introduce the officials is to broaden once again the picture of life as energy.

A. Introducing the Twelve Officials

Imagine we are sitting in a theatre-in-the-round. On the stage before us are four raised platforms — pavilions of a sort. They are arranged in the four directions and bear the appropriate colors; the platform in the South is an impressive red and the others are also brightly colored: blue for the North, green for the East, white for the West. The stage connecting the four directions is a light yellow. We see, once more, the now familiar pattern:

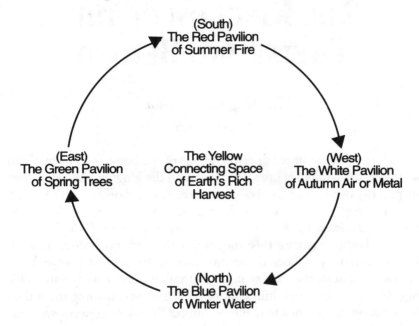

Suddenly, light focuses on the blue pavilion of the North. Music begins; a swirl of mist appears; out of the mist arise two figures dressed in blue robes: *The Minister of Deep Waters and an associate*. Second, the focus shifts to the green pavilion of the East. Again music, swirling mist, and the emergence of two figures dressed in green: *A General and his Aide-de-camp*. Next focus shifts to the white pavilion of the West. Music, mist, and two figures dressed in white: *A First Minister and an associate*.

All eyes rest on the red pavilion. Yet surprisingly, the next happening occurs in the portion of the stage connecting the four pavilions. Suddenly in a burst of yellow, two figures appear dressed in golden

---

robes: *The Ministers of Earth's Bounty and Its Distribution.* Closer to earth, these ministers connect the other pavilions. Attending to basics, they do not obstruct vision. In every way, they facilitate interconnection.

Finally, when all is in readiness, light falls upon the red pavilion. As if stepping out of fire, four figures in red appear: *The Sovereign of Awakened Heart and the Consort (also called Heart Protector), each with an attendant.*[3]

We have watched the twelve officials arise out of the energies of the five elements. They are at one with the elements; they are simply the elements differentiated into more specific functions.

Since we already have experience of the five different energies, we already have some understanding of the officials that arise from them. Yet to keep in mind four officials for summer and two officials each, for the other seasons, seems overwhelming. Let us then simplify.

Let us first acknowledge the twelve players as an ensemble. Then, let the assistants exit. Let even the Consort (or Heart Protector) take temporary leave. Finally, let both Earth ministers also depart for the time being. This will produce a more basic, more manageable arrangement — four officials, one for each direction, each official holding a task or function. Those remaining on stage are the following:

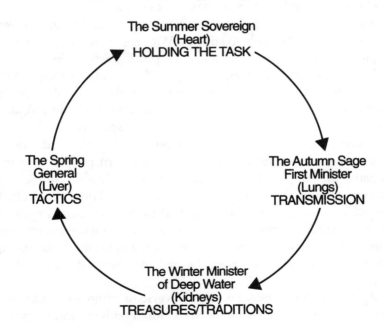

The Summer Sovereign
(Heart)
HOLDING THE TASK

The Autumn Sage
First Minister
(Lungs)
TRANSMISSION

The Winter Minister
of Deep Water
(Kidneys)
TREASURES/TRADITIONS

The Spring
General
(Liver)
TACTICS

In the body as a kingdom, each official holds a role and responsibility. The Sovereign stays focused on the *task* in the widest possible context. The First Minister is concerned with *transmission* — from the heavens through the Sovereign to the people, so that a noble spirit is embodied throughout the kingdom. The Minister of Deep Waters is responsible for the *treasures* and *traditions* of the kingdom. The wily General has responsibility for *tactics*, for remaining adaptable in a constantly changing world.

The South/North axis — Fire to Water (Heart to Kidneys) — deals with the sun and the oceans. The life-giving, light-giving and warmth-giving qualities of fire are from the beginning.[4] The deep waters evoke the ancestry of all life on the planet. Both officials hold and treasure what is ancient and precious.

The East/West axis brings together the First Minister and the General. The First Minister transmits a sense of the task from the heavens to the people in such a way that the task and its spirit are embodied in action. The General, like a master of the martial arts, is ever alert to unexpected dangers and opportunities.

Such is a first glimpse of what the officials are.

B. Creating the Conditions for Proceeding

As we enter more fully into the analogy of body and kingdom, various obstacles are likely to appear. With regard to these obstacles, our guides, Lao Tzu and Confucius, can provide assistance.

First, Lao Tzu might counsel us thus: The officials are archetypes, mysteries to be learned from but never fathomed completely. They are a part of the natural cycles from which they arise. Do not think about them narrowly. Allow them to exist in a larger space of possibility.

Second, Confucius might counsel us thus: Recover what is best in the old to serve the new. I realize that modern people have little sympathy for kings and courts, together with a healthy suspicion of superior-inferior relationships. Yet to see the whole is to see each official as equally important. One can say that each is the most important! When a medical emergency arises and there is urgent need of transport to the hospital, then transportation is the most important. If the garbage piles up in the body (or city), then elimination is the most important, and so on.

Again, Confucius might counsel, diverse function is not inherently patriarchal. The officials as archetypes enfold both yin and yang energies. And functions (such as holding the task) are to be interpreted widely. Let us not, in the name of ideology, be blinded to the significance of simple functions. The large-minded person praises the particular, finds worth in the smallest task, and acknowledges each function fully.

Finally, both Lao Tzu and Confucius might note that *the officials are in us*. The officials point us to the functions and dysfunctions in our own body, mind and spirit. They allow us to live consciously what otherwise might simply be lived in us.

C. THE OFFICIALS IN SOME DETAIL

To continue our discussion, let us bring the Earth officials back on stage, so as to have every element represented. The configuration is as below:

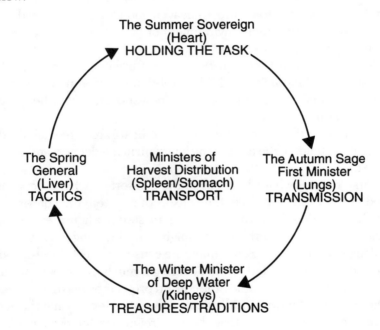

The order of discussion is first along the South-North axis, then the East-West, and finally the Earth ministers in the center.

1. The Sovereign of Awakened Heart

In the kingdom as in the body, the Heart is sovereign and the sovereign is the Heart. As Lao Tzu would stress, the function of the sovereign is to remain open to the inspiration of the heavens — like an empty bowl — in a state of receptive readiness. As Confucius would stress, the function of sovereign emphasizes benevolence (human-heartedness — *jen*).

The sovereign, like a symphony conductor, holds the mission and radiates joyful warmth by example and action.[5] Such a leader is far from the "hegemon" (*pa*) who rules by coercion and deception. Such a leader emulates the function of true king (*wang*) who nourishes life throughout the kingdom and sees that all is ordered well so that the needs of body, heart/mind, and spirit are met. The modern Tibetan teacher, Chogyam Trungpa, stands in this tradition when he says: "When human beings lose their connection to nature, to heaven and earth, then they do not know how to nurture their environment or how to rule their world — which is saying the same thing."[6]

Such is the surprising equation: to nurture one's environment is equivalent to ruling one's world. Thus, rule is not seen primarily in terms of force; leadership is not thought of as "power over," but rather power to give and preserve life.[7]

The other officials in the circle of the heart are three; all aid the Sovereign in holding the tasks of the kingdom in the deepest and widest context.

First, there is what I have called the Consort — what others have called Heart Protector. Like the consort of a queen, the consort of a king, like the double of the heart, this mysterious figure exercises a subtle influence — perhaps, we might say, bringing love to love, speaking heart to heart. Sometimes, the consort protects by absorbing anger and ill-will directed to the Sovereign, much as the pericardium protects the heart. Sometimes, the consort protects by making the heart of the sovereign known to individuals one-to-one, expressing the care, concern and appreciation that the Sovereign has for each person's contribution. In such wise, the Consort becomes a messenger radiating the affection of the Sovereign in a personal manner, while the Sovereign holds full receptivity to the heavens.

Second, there is the Sorter, in another pairing with the Sovereign. This official has features of a modern Chief of Staff for a president, namely, sorting, scheduling, prioritizing and separating the essential

---

from the inessential. This official is crucial if the Sovereign is to think clearly and act wisely. The Sorter also has features of an alchemist, transforming whatever comes to the Sovereign into material of the highest quality for use.

Third in the circle of the heart is an official paired with the Consort. The Consort, as we have seen, expresses care and concern in a very personal way, taking the affection of the Sovereign to members of the kingdom in face to face contacts. Paired with the Consort is an official I will call the Minister for the Conditions of Harmony (the Triple Warmth-Giver). Where the Consort acts personally, the Triple Warmth-Giver acts more impersonally. The concern here is that conditions of warmth are evenly distributed from head to foot, from one end of the commonwealth to the other. Like a gracious host, this minister provides warm and supportive conditions of care wherein all work may be done fully and creatively.

2. The Minister of Deep Waters

The one I call Minister of Deep Waters stands facing the Sovereign — as the waters of earth face the fire of the sun.[8] The waters and the fire face each other in an ancient manner — both being needed for the act of creation. The Minister of Deep Waters preserves the ancestral power — the connection with the earth story and the human story through ancestral energies. This is a ministry that carries and remembers the depth of life. This minister guards the resources needed in the kingdom. We can call this minister a "treasurer" if we think widely enough of all there is to be treasured; if we think, for example, of Japan where artists and craftspersons are named "national treasures."

The associate of the Minister of Deep Waters might be called the Minister of Regional Resources, caring for the treasures and traditions in their diverse homeplaces. Thus, both ministers are guardians of resources — one being wider in scope, the other, more specific.

3. The First Minister

The sagely First Minister and the vigorous General also face each other — as autumn faces spring. It is not a matter of age; as archetypal figures, they are all ages and of no age. We think of both as wise, yet their types of wisdom, like their tasks, differ.

The First Minister — a master in the diplomatic arts — has skills reminiscent of wizards. The wise old woman/wise old man come to mind. The task of the First Minister is to *transmit* the inspiration of the heavens, under the direction of the Sovereign, into the realm of day-to-day communal living. As such, this minister must look to the roots of the matter and understand what is needed to sustain the network of life. In less than ideal circumstances, Chou En Lai often performed well the functions of First Minister for his stormy leader, Chairman Mao Tse Tung.

In the physical body, this function is performed by the energy system associated with the Lungs. The Lungs take inspiration from the heavens and transmit the breath throughout the body. In just such fashion, the First Minister takes the inspiration from the Sovereign of Awakened Heart and sees to its embodiment in the kingdom. This minister also transmits back to the Sovereign the sentiments of the people, the actual impact of policies, etc. Because the First Minister is a transmission conduit in both directions, high skills of courtesy, diplomacy, and wisdom are called for. Like the Lungs, this official takes in and lets go — always so that worth is honored and respect is preserved.

The associate who supports the work of Lungs is Colon. Perhaps we might name this partner of Lungs, the Minister of Letting Go, the Official of Autumn Emptiness. The function of this official is again absolutely essential. The Official of Emptiness is concerned with removing burdens, making space, recycling waste, letting go of what no longer serves. The function of elimination, letting go, giving away — all this is seen so beautifully in the bow. One must empty to receive, create silence to hear, open a vista to see.

I recall the classic story of the Western professor who went to a Japanese Zen Master to learn Zen. The Zen Master received him graciously, poured tea for his guest, and kept pouring until the tea spilled over cup, saucer, and table. "Stop!" the professor cried. "Can't you see that the cup is full?"

"Yes," replied the Zen Master. "This is how you are — so full of opinions — how can I teach you Zen?"

The bow shows Lungs and Colon acting together beautifully. An emptying to receive; a stillness and composure; a deep acknowledgment of self and others.

4. The General

The General — like a forest-dwelling master of the martial arts — is concerned with expecting the unexpected in the defense of life. This official is able to face fear and move life forward. The General is a master of tactics. In the spirit of the martial arts, the more masterful the general is, the less force will be necessary. The path of non-action (*wu wei*) demonstrates profound warriorship in its highest development.

A story is told of a young American student of the martial art called aikido. He is riding on a train near Tokyo. A drunken workman enters the car, raging and railing at everyone. The young American sees his opportunity to test his skills in combat, all in utter righteousness. Before violence meets violence, the drunk is distracted by a frail, old Japanese gentleman, sitting peacefully in his kimono. The elderly Japanese engages the drunk in conversation about saki, about how he and his wife enjoyed taking warm saki in the evening on the bench in their little garden. "You must have a wonderful wife also," the elderly gentleman offered. "I don't got no wife, I don't got no home, I don't got no job. I'm so ashamed of myself," replied the workman, now sobbing deeply.

The young American aikido student had reached his stop, just as the little old man coaxed the drunk to sit by him. The old man was cradling the drunk's head in his lap. The young American had seen aikido practiced in combat by a master and its essence was love.[9]

Just as we had to be weaned of associations of force to think anew of ruling, so we must be weaned of associations of violence to think anew of warriorship.[10]

I picture the General's associate as an aide-de-camp.[11] The function of this minister is wise and effective judgment — a decision-making capacity that matches the type of vision and planning associated with the General. The General's task concerns tactics. The wise and effective judgment called for here suits the General's task. Such decision-making is timely, effective and fair.

5. The Ministers of Harvest Distribution

Thus far, we have introduced four of the twelve officials, each with their accompanying associates. The four stand like the seasons — Sovereign to Minister of Deep Waters as fiery summer to the waters of winter; General to First Minister as spring to autumn. In this configuration, the four are linked through the center. In the center is Earth as a phase of life (harvest); in the center is a blend of all seasons.

Just so, the minister in the center is a minister of transitions — of transit — of transporting the nourishment to all officials and all members of the kingdom. This Minister of Nourishing Exchange provides "food" for all needs.[12] The energy systems are the earth meridians of spleen and stomach — the functions of making available the harvest. The Spleen is called the Minister of Transport; the Stomach, we may call the Minister of Readying Nourishment (also the Official of Rotting and Ripening).

When we see the Earth Ministers in the center, we see clearly the functions of readying nourishment (digesting, putting into useful form), and distributing nourishment.

After this lesson is learned, the earth elements may be returned to their place on the circle of the five seasons. For an illustration of the twelve officials in this five seasons circle, see below.

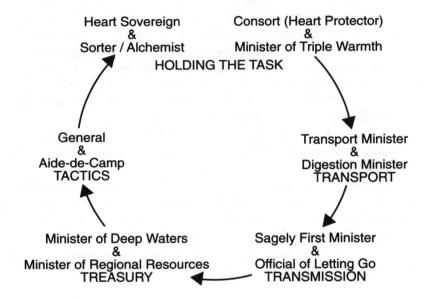

Heart Sovereign
&
Sorter / Alchemist
HOLDING THE TASK

Consort (Heart Protector)
&
Minister of Triple Warmth

General
&
Aide-de-Camp
TACTICS

Transport Minister
&
Digestion Minister
TRANSPORT

Minister of Deep Waters
&
Minister of Regional Resources
TREASURY

Sagely First Minister
&
Official of Letting Go
TRANSMISSION

D. To Come to Life More Fully in the Kingdom of the Twelve

When all twelve functions of the body-mind-spirit are working harmoniously and well, then the kingdom is in good order. Disorder occurs when proper functioning breaks down. Yet we are not without recourse. *The functions are in us; the officials are us — in our functioning.* We are each the Sovereign in our own life and kingdom (however large or small we take our kingdom to be). We are each also First Minister, Master of Strategic Planning, Guardian of Resources, etc. We have access to these powers, which are within. How then do we tend our good functioning?

We are invited — as Sovereigns tending our life and all life — to awaken the heart. We are invited to care for the heart; care for holding and keeping the tasks of life in the widest, most noble context; care for touching and being touched, loving and being loved.

We are invited to practice the diplomatic, communicative skills of the First Minister and the discipline of letting go. As in bowing, acknowledgment and letting go appear together.

We are invited to cherish our resources (and all resources) in the spirit of the Minister of Deep Waters. In such a spirit, nothing need be wasted; all may work together unto good.

We are invited to practice the spirit of the arts of the Martial ministers, noting the dangers and opportunities that life presents, desiring to act in nonaggressive and nonarrogant ways, fostering wise, effective, timely and fair interventions.

We are invited to practice the arts of the Earth ministers, readying and distributing nourishment to all quarters of the commonwealth.

E. THE KINGDOM AND BEYOND

In Part Two, we have seen how one chi energy is differentiated into the aspects of yin and yang, differentiated again into the five phases, and differentiated yet again into the twelve functions. In traditional acupuncture, the twelve officials refer to twelve meridians of energy along which acupuncture points lie. The next natural expansion would be to go from the twelve meridians to the acupuncture points on the meridians. Let us speak figuratively of 360 acupuncture points as matching the 360 degrees in the circle.[13] Therapeutically, this would bring us to consider the 360 points of treatment or, in our case, to the 360 points of service. Imaginatively, this expansion might lead us to consider the earth itself as a kingdom, to move from the body politic to the body planetary.[14] Does this take us to the end of the unfolding? No. There are energies beyond the body, energies beyond the processes of earth. There is the universe itself, what Lao Tzu calls "the ten thousand things." And moving in and through the energy in all its differentiation is the mysterious Tao, as enfolding all things.[15]

To summarize: In Part Two, the movement was from small to large, from the one as center through the two, the five, the twelve, and thence to hint at still further differentiations — the 360 points, the ten thousand things, unto a glimpse of the one as the encompassing presence throughout the universe. Part Two's movement was *from small to large, from center to circumference*.

Part Three's design takes us *from large to small, from circumference to the center*. However, rather than focusing on the time of archetypal and recurring cycles, Part Three focuses on the timespans of novel and surprising changes. In this next part, we shall explore *life as dwelling* and come to understand the seven domains.

Notes

[1] Plato in the Republic draws out the analogy between parts of the person to parts of the polis (city-state). Traditional Chinese medicine, as we shall see shortly, speaks (in the *Nei Ching*) of the twelve functional meridians as twelve officials. The New Testament (I Corinthians, 12) speaks of one body with many members and draws the analogy between the physical body and the community of the faithful as the Body of Christ.

[2] See mention in chapter two. Also see Claude Larre and Elisabeth Rochat De La Vallée, *Huang Di Nei Jing Su Wen, Chapter 8, The Secret Treatise of the Spiritual Orchid*, unrevised transcript of a seminar transcribed and edited by Peter Firebrace (East Grinstead, East Sussex, England: British Register of Oriental Medicine, 1985).

[3] I take liberties here. The Sovereign is immediately flanked with what is often called the Heart Protector, and even more mysteriously, in the *Nei Ching* as Tan Zhong. However, the idea of consort shows up explicitly in Tibetan Buddhism. For the seven gifts of the universal monarch, see Chogyam Trungpa, *Shambhala: The Sacred Path of the Warrior* (Boulder, CO: Shambhala, 1984), chapter eighteen.

[4] In evoking the sun as symbol of life and light and warmth, I echo an ancient theme. For a Western formulation see Dante's *Divine Comedy* on the Trinity and its polar opposite; for an Eastern view, see Chogyam Trungpa, *Shambhala*, on Great Eastern Sun.

[5] Warren Bellows and Nancy Post, in their work, call the Heart Official "the conductor." For further information, see Nancy Post's 1989 workbook, *Working Balance: Energy Management for Personal and Professional Well-Being*, privately printed and available through Post Enterprises, Alden Park Manor, Suite 604B, Philadelphia, PA, 19144.

[6] See Chogyam Trungpa, *Shambhala*, p. 132.

7. For Lao Tzu, on leadership, see John Heider, *The Tao of Leadership: Lao Tzu's Tao Te Ching Adapted for a New Age* (New York: Bantam Books, 1986). For Confucius on leadership and force, see David L. Hall and Roger T. Ames, *Thinking Through Confucius* (Albany, NY: State University of New York Press, 1987), chapter three. On two senses of power, see Riane Eisler, *The Chalice and the Blade* (San Francisco: Harper and Row, 1988), esp. chapter eight.

8. The energy system connected with this minister is that of the Kidneys. The association is to the reservoirs, the reserves, the resources, of life.

9. The story, which comes from Terry Dobson, is told in wonderful detail in Ram Dass and Gorman, *How Can I Help?*, pp. 167-171.

10. See *Shambhala*, on a redefinition of warrior. Trungpa's emphasis on the warrior as courageous is reminiscent also of Plato in *The Republic* where the human soul is composed of a rational element, a spirited element and the appetites. The virtue of the spirited part is courage.

11. The energetic system here is associated with Gallbladder.

12. See Ken Wilber, *A Sociable God* (Boulder, CO: Shambhala, 1983), chapter four, on mana at each level.

13. Although there are over 360 acupuncture points on various meridians of the body, my symbolic sense was delighted that in J. R. Worsley's *Traditional Chinese Acupuncture: Vol. I: Meridians and Points* (Tisbury, Wiltshire, England: Element Books Ltd., 1982), Dr. Worsley lists exactly 361 points (360 + a center point?). See Appendix 21: Names of the Points (listed alphabetically), pp. 304-07.

14. See chapter ten on the institutional domain, where this suggestion is worked out more fully.

15. In Part One, chapter three, I suggested an analogy with a flower opening in the morning and closing in the evening. Part Two follows the outward arc from the one to the many. We have not explored the inward arc from the many to the one, although we have kept with us Lao Tzu as a reminder of the meditative way of simplification, and we shall treat the need for meditative awareness in Part Four.

LIFE AS DWELLING

The World as Seven Domains

THE IMAGE:
CONCENTRIC CIRCLES ON THE
SURFACE OF THE LAKE

Imagine the lake surrounded by mountains. The sun rises; the mists burn away. The lake lies placid on a warm summer's day. Two children come to the shore and begin to toss stones into the water from the bank. Watch as a stone hits the water. Watch the ripples become concentric circles, each circle beginning in the center and moving to the periphery. Suppose a photographer were to stop the motion. Suppose we now see *a small center circle, five rings and an encompassing context*. Let the encompassing context — the photo itself — stand for the seventh "circle." I shall call these circles *domains* and distinguish seven nested domains — seven concentric circles.[1] As we shall see, the first and seventh circles are most mysterious and, in fact, have some analogous features.

A domain, as I define it, is a spatio-temporal context in which humans (and others) can consciously dwell.

The domains give us a picture of the world as frames of time and modes of (potential) community. Moving from the center outward, the timeframes and communities appear as follows:

TIMEFRAME	MODE OF "POTENTIAL" COMMUNITY
1. The Moment	"Community" of one person; diversity/unity within one person
2. The Lifetime	Community of two — seen best as community of two friends
3. Generations	Community of a family over at least three generations
4. Centuries	Structured communities of institutions; network of same
5. Millennia	Cultural communities/ cultural epochs - story of humankind
6. Aeons	The community of all living beings on the Planet Earth
7. Time beyond time	All beings in the Tao

We are always in these nested times and hold membership in many communities concurrently.

A. THE DOMAINS ARE INTERWOVEN

The domains are interwoven; they are nested without being hierarchical. Consider the image of the concentric circles of water on the lake. Moving from large to small can be as appropriate as moving from small to large. More encompassing is not better in any absolute sense. We can move from context to context as required. We can expand our vision, our sense of time, the scope of our identifications. We can condense, focus and incarnate vision in each of the distinctive contexts of life.

B. THE DOMAINS ARE BOTH CONTEXT AND PROCESS

All but the seventh domain are particular subpatterns of the total pattern. Each subpattern can be seen as a *context* (defined by the subjects/structures in a "spatial" sense) and a *process* (as defined by the associated scale of time). Domains have both aspects. Appreciating the temporal or process aspect is valuable to wean us from thinking of the domains (or ourselves in them) as static *things*.[2]

In Domain One, I am my bodily self in moment-to-moment time. However, I am also much more. In Domain Two, I am the sum of all the interpersonal relationships over my life to date. In Domain Three, I am also a unique summation of my family history. In Domain Four, I play a part in the temporal life of the institutions I serve. In Domain Five, I am a crystallization of the historical time of my nation and of the unfolding of my species' story. In Domain Six, I am part of earth processes of some 4.5 billion years, and I realize that earth's story is but a phase of the cosmic story. The elements in my hand, as Brian Swimme points out, are born of stars and originated some 14 billion years ago.[3] Since the domains are nested, each moment of mine is a moment in my lifetime, family time, institutional time, cultural time, planetary and cosmic time. I am different ages in different domains.

C. The Domains and Coming to Life More Fully

In this book, all of our explorations are for the sake of coming to life more fully so as to serve life more wisely and more nobly. Our two guides, Lao Tzu and Confucius, are reminders of our quest for sagely stillness within and sovereign service without. This was our aim in Part Two ("Life as Energy"); this is still our aim in Part Three ("Life as Dwelling").

Since we had a healing intent when exploring the world as energy, we took, as our basis, the worldview underlying traditional Chinese medicine. Our speaking of energy (yin-yang, five elements, twelve officials) was based on the polarities, rhythms and functions in the body-mind-spirit of the individual patient.

Who is this patient? Is it simply a person in domains one and two? Or can we speak of healing in wider contexts? Do the principles of energy also apply in the domain of family and institution? May we speak of the balance and imbalance, the good and poor functioning, of culture and planet?

Questions such as these led me to consider the possibility of distinguishing and examining a set of contexts — a set of domains in which we can come to life more fully. Precedent for doing this can be found in the Confucian tradition.[4]

Distinguishing the domains will help us to identify the patient — to see where and what kind of treatment is needed. Furthermore, the notion of nested domains is itself a strong antidote to the isolated individualism that has become so much a characteristic of our age.[5] The nested domains remind us that a person is more than "a skin-encapsulated ego"[6] (a caricature of identity in Domain One). The nested domains remind us that healing is more than the interaction of two such "skin encapsulated egos" (a caricature of Domain Two). Alternatively, distinguishing domains aids us to recognize when there is collapsing of domains, for example, when the institutional domain is collapsed into the interpersonal domain, and social issues are reduced to purely personal ones.

Seeing the domains one by one will allow us to see how *each is in us* and *we are in each*. Seeing the domains as interwoven will allow us to understand contextual differences within a prior unity.

A practical corollary is that, when a possibility opens on any level, it shifts the energy, thus opening possibility at all other levels.

Within each domain, we can move

From	the many, the fragmented	*To*	the one, the whole
From	separateness	*To*	connection
From	being detached	*To*	being involved
From	standing as an outsider	*To*	being identified with the domain
From	inferior mind	*To*	superior mind

Within each domain, we have choices. We can "relate to" a domain or we can find that "we are the domain." Each domain is a potential communion.[7]

Consider again the image of the concentric rings in the water. In this part, we shall move from the outermost ring to the center, the order used in the following chart.

THE SEVEN DOMAINS —
SEVEN CONTEXTS WITH ASSOCIATED TIMEFRAMES

7) THE DOMAIN OF MYSTERY —
    WITHIN AND BEYOND TIME
The circle whose center is everywhere; whose circumference, nowhere.

6) THE PLANET EARTH DOMAIN—
    COSMIC TIME: AEONS

This is a domain where the human is situated in *the more than human* — where we come to realize our kinship with the animals, plants and elements of our shared earth. Also, we are coming to see the earth as a self-organizing, self-developing organism. Earth's story is embedded in the cosmic story. Consider these six cosmic periods (modified from Berry): (i) from the Fireball to the elements and galaxies, (ii) from the Milky Way to our solar system, (iii) earth in its physical formation, (iv) the emergence of plant life, (v) the emergence of (conscious) animal life, and (vi) the formation of the human and the development of the cultural epochs.

5) THE CULTURAL DOMAIN — THE TIME OF THE HUMAN RACE: MILLENNIA

Culture is seen as that set of meanings, values, purposes, myths and rituals that establish the common sense of reality for a people. Today, we think of the *nation* as the prime carrier of culture (and we recognize sub-cultures within the nation). We acknowledge national culture as the foreground; we emphasize the *history of the race* as background. In particular, we find useful Thomas Berry's notion of five cultural epochs: the paleolithic, the neolithic-tribal, the classical, the technological, and the new emerging ecological epoch.

4) THE INSTITUTIONAL DOMAIN — THE TIME OF NATIONS: CENTURIES

Particular *institutions* (e.g. governmental and economic, religious and educational) are part of a *system of institutions*. This interlocking system presently constitutes the nation state.

3) THE (THREE GENERATIONAL) FAMILY DOMAIN — THE TIME OF GENERATIONS

When we have children (or accept responsibility for "the children"), the time of generations opens up for us. We come to think of our generation, our parents' generation, and our children's generation. We see how the gifts and wounds of family history arise and are passed on.

2) THE (1-TO-1) RELATIONAL DOMAIN — THE TIME OF THE LIFETIME

Here we see the dynamics of pairs, of interactions across a range from enemy to stranger to neighbor to friend to beloved.

Round about adolescence, we begin to have a sense of our lifetime. Our past becomes problematic; our future, uncertain. So it is with others also. With this new sense of time and identity, we have a greater capacity both for manipulation and for friendship.

1) THE PERSONAL DOMAIN
   THE TIME OF THE MOMENT
   From the "now" of the child through the "now" of dispersed emotions to the "now" of the sage — the sphere of "inner work."

Notes

[1] As mentioned earlier, seven domains is a manageable set. One could, no doubt, distinguish further — for example, particular institutions and the network of institutions, particular cultures within an epoch, bioregions and their interrelationship to form the earth, and again planetary history and universe history. However, seven domains give sufficient scope to integrate insights from the Western social sciences and from the Chinese classics.

[2] For an excellent critique of the modern West's propensity to "thing-ifying" everything, see Alan W. Watts, *Nature, Man and Woman* (New York: Random House, 1970), 1st published 1958.

[3] See Swimme, *The Universe is a Green Dragon.*

[4] Among the classics, see especially *The Great Learning* (quoted in part in chapter thirteen of this work) and the *I Ching.* See also Thomas Berry, "Affectivity in Classical Confucian Tradition," in his aforementioned *Riverdale Papers on China.*

[5] Critiques of one-sided autonomy and isolated individualism are many and varied. For Habermas and the Frankfort school, see Thomas McCarthy, *The Critical Theory of Jürgen Habermas* (Cambridge, MA: The MIT Press, 1981). For a nodal point in the modern feminist critique, see Carol Gilligan, *In a Different Voice: Psychological Theory and Women's Development* (Cambridge, MA: Harvard University Press, 1982). Also note Alasdair MacIntyre, *After Virtue: A Study in Moral Theory* (Notre Dame: University of Notre Dame Press, 1981), and Robert Bellah, Richard Madsen, William Sullivan, Ann Swidler and Steven Tipton, *Habits of the Heart* (New York: Harper and Row, 1986).

[6] The phrase is from Alan Watts.

[7] This theme will be developed in Part Four.

CHAPTER SEVEN

DOMAIN SEVEN: THE MYSTERIOUS TAO

Like the empty sky it has no boundaries
Yet it is right in this place, ever profound and clear.
When you seek to know it, you cannot see it.
You cannot take hold of it,
But you cannot lose it.
In not being able to get it, you get it.
When you are silent, it speaks;
When you speak, it is silent.
The great gate is wide open to bestow alms,
And no crowd is blocking the way.

— *Cheng-Tao Ke*[1]

We begin in paradox. What is "no-where" is also "now-here."[2] What is more vast than universes is also in the mustard seed, at the core of our being, the soul of our soul.

I spoke earlier of growing up on the island of Aquidneck in Narragansett bay. There are times when the fog sweeps in from the Atlantic when the entire city fades; boundaries blur; horizons are lost. Things arise before you as if from a void. You could be anywhere, nowhere. If you grow up there, the sound of foghorns marks you for life.

When my father died, I had already been living in North Carolina for some years. I flew home the next day through a clear blue April sky, and as the plane descended over the waters for a landing in Boston's Logan airport, the sun shimmered on the water, a thousand mirrors of light reflected off the rippling sea. I experienced my father then — what he had risen from, what he was a part of, what he returned to. There, for a moment, was a sense of something vast — containing the son in the father and the father in the son. The plane landed smoothly. Relatives were there to meet me and drive me home. I told no one. The funeral lay ahead, yet I had already celebrated my father's life and death — there in the plane above the ocean on a bright April day.

To attempt to speak of the Tao is an instant demonstration that you are a fool, a child, a lover or a sage. Or, since children and sages, lovers and fools have much in common, the attempt may simply reveal that you are human — a center of awareness suspended between everything and nothing, between living and dying.

The Tao is the way. The Great Mystery. That which is before the beginning and after the end and everywhere in the process. At the cosmic level, it is the Invisible Pattern, which connects all. It is the canvas before the master calligrapher draws the Great Circle — and it is the brush and the circle and all else besides. It is the silence before the first note — and it is the singer and the song.

The first chapter of Lao Tzu's great classic, the *Tao Te Ching*, says: "The Tao that can be spoken is not the eternal Tao."[3] How can this be grasped?

Jay Williams tells us that there are but two routes available to approach the unapproachable, to speak the unspeakable: the route of *neti, neti* (not this, not that) and the route of myth.[4]

The *path of neti, neti* is the path of denial. The Tao is neither this nor that, not a thing nor a process, not subjective nor objective, not existence nor non-existence. And it should be said: the Tao is not properly a domain either. Consider the things we see and touch and hear and feel. Consider the attributes we give to such phenomena, then relentlessly deny that such attributes are properly applied to the Tao. In the East, the master of the way of denial was Nargarjuna, and the mode of denial became a stock in trade of many Buddhist thinkers. So much so that we have the joke: Question: How many Buddhist monks does it take to change a light bulb? Answer: Two — one to turn it and one not to turn it.

In the West, the *way of neti, neti* was known as the *via negativa*. Such a negative way does indeed safeguard the realm of mystery. Yet it only tells us what the Tao is *not*. In so doing, it walks many steps with the agnostic. Eventually, the path of *neti, neti* ends in silence. "That of which one cannot speak, of that one must be silent." This was the conclusion of the early Wittgenstein's *Tractatus*.[5] Lao Tzu, the legendary author of the *Tao Te Ching*, would have smiled agreement.

If the Tao is beyond distinctions, beyond dualism of any kind, then the route of *neti, neti* is instructive in its own chaste manner. For language and speech exist by carving up the world into this and that, making distinctions and drawing contrasts. The net of language is inherently dualistic. However fine one makes the mesh on the net, the Tao is not a fish to be so caught.

Yet the fool and the child babble; the lover and the artist seek to express their love; the sage, by doing and not-doing, teaches. Here, we encounter the second mode of speaking the unspeakable: *the way of myth*.

Myth begins in metaphor. What I experience is like this, . . . but not quite. What I experienced in the plane flying to my father's funeral took its occasion from the sun glinting on the choppy sea. The crests were individual and they were part of the one sea; they were momentarily brilliantly shining in the sun, transfigured and they were nothing special. What of my father and me was like that? This is how I speak it. I see one "thing" *as* "something else." Something universal makes itself manifest in this particular, and something very particular makes itself manifest in this universal occurrence. Yet I cannot convey what the one "thing" is, nor what the "something else" is, apart from more of the same symbolic, associational, evocative language.[6] To be sure, any attempt is insufficient, but to exchange poetry for prose, the metaphoric for the literal, is more ridiculous still.

So we use metaphors and move to story and parable and then to myth and ritual. This is the way of myth. The Zen masters speak of certain symbols, certain stories, as "a finger pointing to the moon." When the finger is worshipped for itself, then one ceases to follow it as a pointer to something more, to another — more expansive — reality or another dimension of this reality, which is our world.

Shakespeare has Hamlet say: "There are more things in heaven and earth, Horatio, than are dreamt of in your philosophy."[7] So it is with the symbolic. We hear the story and we hear something more — not apart from but in the story, belonging to the story in its fullness. Asked to speak it, we can only tell another story or return to silence.

What is the Great Mystery? One medieval mystic in the West likened it to a circle whose center is everywhere and whose circumference is nowhere. One medieval mystic in the East — the author of the Oxherding Pictures — drew a circle. The eighth picture — where once the series ended — is just this: a circle drawn with rough brush on empty paper. Its title: "The Ox and the oxherd have been forgotten." Is this the Tao? It is and it isn't. Once the brush touches paper and the circle is drawn, then foreground and background arise. Again, there is duality. What cannot be said cannot be drawn either. Better to say, along the path of myth, that we offer here an image of the Tao, a finger pointing to the moon.

A. THE SPACIOUS AND THE SPECIAL

The Tao is both vast and simple. Meditation points to the Tao as one senses a spaciousness in the mind wherein particular thoughts come and go. Certain paintings and certain poems point to the Tao. I think of this haiku by Hashin:

> No sky at all;
> no earth at all — and still
> the snowflakes fall. . . .[8]

Such art sensitizes us to the depth of life, in simple and evocative ways. Raymond Smullyan speaks of experiencing Taoism as "a state of inner serenity combined with an intense aesthetic awareness."[9] Indeed, the Tao is present in the particular flower, or sunset, or face of the loved one. The Tao is very concrete, right before us, touched in what we touch.

The Mahayana Buddhists speak of *sunyata* and *tathata*. *Sunyata* is the emptiness, the spaciousness, the vastness, the fertile void wherein all possibilities are present. *Tathata* is the suchness of things. Suppose that you have had a near death experience. You awaken in profound joy and gratitude. The taste of orange juice, the smell of flowers, the sight of a loved one's familiar face, the touch of your child's hand — all are seen with a freshness that is like being here/now at the morning of creation.

B. THE TAO AND THEOS

I have echoed Jay Williams' warning that we only speak of mystery using the *way of neti, neti* and the *way of myth*. The way of denial (not this, not that) reminds us that we cannot speak of the Totality in the language of duality and separateness. Myth as used here is not false-hood; it is a story that points to the mystery. In playful manner, I would say that myth is as dangerous as dynamite and points to T-N-T — to the True Nature of Things and to Tao/Theos - Now - Transformation.

To use the Chinese word Tao is useful; not knowing the word, we are open to hear what the mystery might be like. To use the Greek word *Theos* in place of the more familiar word "God" can provide like service; not knowing the word, we are open to hear what the mystery might be like.

In the *Tao Te Ching*, Lao Tzu speaks of the Tao and the ten thousand things. The ten thousand things refer to all of visible, tangible, sensible reality — the world as we encounter it. The Tao, we can say, is not one of the ten thousand things; it is not the ten thousand and first thing; it is not a thing at all.

In the religions of the Book (Judaism, Christianity, and Islam), one speaks of *Theos* as creator, and all of the visible, tangible, sensible reality as creatures or the created things. *Theos*, we may say, is not one more of the created things; *Theos* is not a created thing; *Theos* is not a thing at all.[10]

Of course, there are differences. As a sample, the Tao is not spoken of as creator; *Theos* is. The Tao is regarded more impersonally — more like "the force" of Star Wars. One comes into harmony with the Tao. *Theos* is regarded more like a person, having will and understanding. One can obey or disobey *Theos*. And yet, in the mystic tradition, serving *Theos* is far beyond reward/punishment and the obedience so sug-gested. "I will not serve God like a laborer, in expectation of my wages," said Rabia, the Sufi saint.[11] And as Raymond Smullyan reminds us, "the better you get to know something, the more personal it becomes."[12]

What I am suggesting is this: the mystic tradition is experiential and moves at a level beneath creed, code and cult, beneath arguments about transcendence or immanence. The mystic tradition is at home with the playful and paradoxical. Consider the mystic tradition of Judaism and think of Martin Buber's *Tales of the Hasidim*.[13] Consider the mystic tradition of Christianity and think, for example, of Eckhart, Hildegard of Bingen, Julian of Norwich. Consider the mystic tradition of Islam and think of Sufis like Jelaluddin Rumi and the marvelous Nasrudin. Consider the Zen tradition in China and Japan. Here, the differences melt and we stand together in respect for the sacredness of all that is. Nor is the notion of unfolding mystery foreign to the great scientists. "I do not know what I may appear to the world," Isaac Newton remarked in his old age, "but to myself I seem to have been only like a boy playing on the seashore, and diverting myself in now and then finding a smoother pebble or a prettier shell than ordinary, whilst the great ocean of truth lay all undiscovered before me."[14]

C. The Tao of Lao Tzu and the Tao of Confucius

Lao Tzu is concerned with the natural world in its unfolding; Confucius is concerned with the human world in its unfolding.

Lao Tzu's *Tao Te Ching* is the classic of the Tao and the Te. Hall and Ames speak of Tao and Te as field and focus. The term "Te" — often translated as virtue or power — is here considered as "the presencing of a particular." The whole — the Tao — the field of possibilities unfolding — is made present in the particular, and the particulars in their unfolding interrelationships are the field that is the Tao.[15] To speak in this manner is already a carrying forward of Lao Tzu's insights. Indeed, Lao Tzu speaks of the processes of nature and the spontaneousness of the Tao. But we are inclined to read these processes as cyclically repeating. How wonderful to see the Tao also as surprising, as an artist or poet can surprise us.

Confucius was less drawn to the cosmic/religious arena. When his student, Chi-lu, asked how the spirits of the dead and the gods should be served, Master K'ung replied, "You are not able even to serve man. How can you serve the spirits?" When Chi-lu asked about death, the Master said: "You do not understand even life. How can you understand death?"[16]

The historical/cultural context provided background to Confucius' social/political concerns. Confucius speaks of the Tao of the sage-rulers, and the Tao of the Duke of Chou. This may account for one of Confucius' most striking sayings: "It is man who is capable of broadening the Tao. It is not the Tao that is capable of broadening man."[17]

To become a superior or exemplary person (*chün tzu*), one must appreciate the resources of the past and the needs of the present in such a way that past insights can become new possibilities for present situations. In this manner, the exemplary person builds bridges and so extends the way. Here, the Tao, far from being a predetermined pattern, is a set of resources and directionalities that call for creative appropriation and creative adaptation. In the words of Master K'ung: "He who by reanimating the old can contribute to the new is indeed worthy of being called a teacher." [18]

At this point, we can put the insights of both sages together. Confucius' emphasis on the role of humans in the unfolding of the human story affords an opening. The Tao is not a fixed pattern, but an open-ended mystery wherein novelty and surprise are possible and prized. Still, the human is indeed birthed from and a part of nature. Lao Tzu's strong deference to the natural world deepens the Confucian notion of understanding the past to contribute to the future. In our own language, we can point out that there is a wisdom at the biological/genetic/ecological level that is more ancient than the human and is most needed in our times.

What, then, is it to dwell in the Tao? Perhaps to be present to all the times of life in the simplicity of the timeless moment. Perhaps this is what R. H. Blyth calls Zen as Zen, that is "the spontaneous, individually created *timeless activity in time* of an undivided mind-body."[19] If so, then the Tao lies at the depth of each domain of life, as the Tao lies at the source of the energies of life. Truly, each domain is vast in its possibility and precious in its particularity. Yet perhaps nowhere do we sense the great pattern so powerfully as in "Ocean-Earth," our home planet. For us, the Earth domain is the first image of the Tao in time and form — the first image and concrete reminder of a web of life more vast than ourselves, more ancient than the human ones.

Notes

[1] The quote is found in Alan Watts *The Way of Zen* (New York: Random House, 1957), p. 145.

[2] I first encountered this word play in Frederick Franck's *Pilgrimage to Now/Here* (Maryknoll, NY: Orbis Books, 1974).

[3] This classic has been translated numerous times. For beginning students, I recommend Lao Tzu, *Tao Te Ching*, a new translation by Gia-Fu Feng and Jane English (New York: Random House Vintage Books, 1972) because the text and photography are so beautifully done. Also consulted in this work are *The Way of Life According to Lao Tzu* by Witter Bynner (New York: Putnam Publishing Perigee Book, 1944); Lao Tzu, *Tao Teh Ching*, trans. John C.H. Wu (New York: St. John's University Press, 1961); Henry Wei, *The Guiding Light of Lao Tzu: A New Translation and Commentary on the Tao Teh Ching* (Wheaton, Ill.: Theosophical Publishing House, Quest Book, 1982) and *Tao*

Te Ching: A New English Version by Stephen Mitchell (New York: Harper and Row, 1988).

4   See Jay G. Williams, *Yeshua Buddha* (Wheaton, IL: Theosophical Publishing House, Quest Book, 1978).

5   See Ludwig Wittgenstein, *Tractatus Logico-Philosophicus* (New York: Humanities Press, 1961).

6   For a Western view of these matters, see David Burrell, *Analogy and Philosophical Language* (New Haven: Yale University Press, 1973).

7   *Hamlet*, act I, scene 5.

8   The translation is by Harold Henderson, quoted in Nancy Wilson Ross, *The World of Zen*, (New York: Random House, 1960), p. 259.

9   See Raymond M. Smullyan, *The Tao is Silent* (New York: Harper and Row, 1977), p. xi.   Smullyan, a logician in the spirit of Lewis Carroll, is also delightful in discussing whether the Tao exists.

10 For an excellent approach to *Theos*, see Jay Williams, *Yeshua Buddha*, chapter one.

11 See Arthur J. Deikman, *The Observing Self: Mysticism and Psychotherapy* (Boston: Beacon Press, 1982), p.77.   The entire chapter where this appears (seven) is a gem.

12 See Smullyan, *The Tao is Silent*, p. 102-03.

13 See Martin Buber, *Tales of the Hasidim: The Early Masters*, trans. Olga Marx (New York: Schocken, 1947) and *Tales of the Hasidim: The Later Masters*, trans. Olga Marx (New York: Schocken, 1948).

14 See David Brewster, *Memoirs of the Life, Writings and Discoveries of Sir Isaac Newton* (Edinburgh: Constable, 1855), vol. II, p. 407.   Quoted in John S. Dunne, *Time and Myth* (New York: Doubleday, 1973), Preface.

15 See Hall and Ames, *Thinking Through Confucius*, p. 216 ff.

16 See *Analects*, XI/12.   Unless otherwise indicated, I am using Confucius, *The Analects* (Lun yü), trans. D.C. Lau, (New York: Viking Penguin, 1979).

17 *Analects* XV:29.

18 See *Analects* II:11.   The rendering is mine.

19 See Frederick Franck, ed., *Zen and Zen Classics: Selections from R.H. Blyth* (New York: Random House, 1978), p. 166.

CHAPTER EIGHT

THE EARTH DOMAIN: BRINGING LIFE TO LIFE

Heaven is my father and earth is my mother
and even such a small creature as I
find an intimate place in its midst.
That which extends throughout the universe,
I regard as my body.
That which directs the universe,
I regard as my nature.
All people are my brothers and sisters
and all things are my companions.

— West Wall Inscription from the office of Chang Tsai,
an 11th-century administrator in China [1]

According to Lao Tzu, the Tao is best seen in the processes of nature. The natural world — with its minerals, plants, animals and humans — in its cyclical, life-sustaining processes is today called the biosphere or ecosphere. This — our home planet — is the earth or planetary domain.

For more than twenty years now, we have had photographs of the earth from space. These hauntingly beautiful photographs show our planet *as a whole*, azure-green in color and enveloped by its swirling, cloud-carrying atmosphere. We now see, in the round, what Lao Tzu considered the first manifestation of the Tao. This encounter with earth as a whole is powerful and poignant.

A. The Earth as a Timespan Longer Than the Time of the Human Species

Recall that a domain is a spatiotemporal context for dwelling.

The spatial context of the earth domain can be seen in the picture of the earth from space. This image of earth is already something of an icon for our age, a mandala for the closing of the twentieth century. Here is the spatial reality — our home planet, a place to live and a living place.

But the earth domain is also a temporal context. The earth has a life. What the astronauts saw and photographed on a specific year, 1969, was some 4.5 billion years in the making. Furthermore, the earth's story is part of a larger story — the unfolding of the cosmos or universe. The cosmic story unfolds over some 15 billion years.

The story of the universe   —   c. 15 billion years,
includes the story of earth   —   c. 4.5 billion years.

Earth is ancient indeed, and yet earth's story occupies only one-third of the timespan of the universe.

In summary, the sixth domain is the domain of earth. The context is the earth as a whole including its bioregions and all life forms within them; the process is the time period of earth in its formation — a time-span of some 4.5 billion years. The background context is the universe; the background process, the unfolding of the universe from the Great Fireball to the present — some 15 billion years.[2]

Extending the schema of Thomas Berry, I propose six cosmic epochs for the sixth domain — six epochs to show the earth's story as backgrounded by the cosmic story.

Six Cosmic Epochs:[3]
1. From the Fireball to the formation of elements and galaxies
2. From the formation of the Milky Way galaxy to the formation of our solar system

3. The earth in its physical and early Gaian formation
   [the micro-organisms, the land, the waters, and the air in their
   life-sustaining cycles]
4. The earth giving birth to more complex plant life
5. The earth giving rise to conscious animal life
6. The earth in its mode of human being and becoming

We notice that the earth in its temporal unfolding is not separate from what it has brought forth. We acknowledge the earth in all its systems (land, water, fire, air; plant, animal, human life).

We see earth as evolving over some 4.5 billion years. We note that the human species is only a million or so years old, that the human part of earth's story is the briefest of the six chapters. Here is a timespan much longer than the time of the human species.

B. THE EARTH AS A COMMUNITY LARGER THAN THE HUMAN COMMUNITY

Think again of the stone thrown into the lake. There is a center, five concentric rings, and an encompassing context. The circumference and the center (domains Seven and One) are especially mysterious, because both the Tao and the deepest sense of self take us to a place of profound oneness. In the other domains — the five interior rings between the deep self as center and the Tao as circumference — we can operate more easily because here there is a clearer sense of self, of others, and of that which connects us.

In each of the inner five domains, there is a community. Here, I use the term "community" widely to mean a unified group of individuals, human and/or nonhuman, that dwells together in a domain (together with any organizing structures specific to that domain). *That* individuals dwell together thus makes them a community in this bare sense; *how* they dwell together — whether selfishly or compassionately, destructively or constructively, superficially or deeply — is another matter. When I wish to speak of a community that reaches a certain degree of harmony, I shall use the term "communion." In my terminology, each of the inner five domains is a community; each has the potential to become a communion.

What is the community of the earth domain? Its scope encompasses the human but goes beyond the human story. Consider the scope of this step by step. Earth's community is larger than the community of two friends, larger than the intergenerational community of family. Earth's community is larger than the community of a nation with its interlocking institutions over a timespan of centuries, larger even than the community of the human race that extends over millennia. All these communal forms of life are limited to the human. Earth's community goes beyond the human. *Earth's community includes all the life forms and the ecosystems of which they are part over the 4.5 billion years of earth's unfolding!*

The key is to shift our thinking from

Anthropocentrism (a human-centered stance)

to

Biocentrism (an all-living-species-centered stance)
or Ecocentrism (an earth-centered stance).

The compassionate response is *to identify with and to respect the intrinsic worth of all beings within the web of earth as ecosystem and, in fact, to identify with and respect earth itself in its functional integrity.*

C. THE EARTH AS GAIA

When James Lovelock began to consider the planet itself as a life form, he needed a name. His friend and fellow-villager, the novelist William Goulding, suggested the name Gaia after the Greek earth goddess. Lovelock and his colleague, life scientist Lynn Margulis, define Gaia as "a complex entity involving the earth's biosphere [life on the surface of the planet], atmosphere, oceans and soil; the totality constituting a feedback or cybernetic system which seeks an optimal physical and chemical environment for life on the planet."[4]

Just as the city-state or kingdom (body politic) can be seen on analogy with the human body (body personal), so now the planet as a whole (body planetary) can likewise be seen on analogy with the human body (and other self-regulating systems). The earth domain is structured as a self-sustaining system and that structure predates humans.

In the poet Dante, we see a shift of centers from earth as center to God as center. Today, we are experiencing a shift from humans as center to earth as center (where earth is also regarded as the primary revelation, the first manifestation of the sacred). Thomas Berry again and again makes primary the evolving earth as creative, self-sustaining subject.

For example, he writes that . . .

> the earth is itself
> the primary physician,
> primary lawgiver,
> primary revelation of the divine,
> primary scientist,
> primary technologist,
> primary commercial venture,
> primary artist,
> primary educator, and
> primary agent in whichever other activity
> we find in human affairs.[5]

What does earth reveal in our day? That we are grounded "in the dynamics of the earth as a self-emerging, self-sustaining, self-educating, self-governing, self-healing, and self-fulfilling community of all the living and nonliving beings of the planet."[6]

The insight that we are all part of one evolving planetary ecosystem comes from modern science; the realization that all beings of the earth are interconnected is a far more ancient one. Even today, many still share a deep conviction that we can learn from the earth, that the wider and older community of all our kin can instruct us yet.

For millennia, in Paleolithic and Neolithic times, there were matricentric cultures worshipping earth as mother and seeing power as the power to give and sustain life.[7] Also many native peoples in the tribal, patricentric epoch dwelled on earth in conscious interconnection with the elements — earth, fire, water and air — as well as with the plants, the animals and the other humans. And yet, as early as the Neolithic period, patriarchal hunting and herding peoples came to conquer by the blade and conceived of power as domination backed by the capacity to take life. Power as control continued through the classical epoch and into the modern industrial, technological epoch. The trend of humans to see themselves as separate and superior to nature accelerated, notwithstanding the voices of poets, prophets, mystics and saints across the ages.

D. To Love the Earth

Imagine that the invitation is always the same: to love self and others and that which connects us.[8] Imagine that we are called to love ourselves, others and that which connects us — in each of the interior five domains. In regard to the earth domain, I shall discuss the urgency, the difficulty and the possibility of responding to this call.

1. The Urgency of Loving the Earth: Cries of Suffering

Today, one need not be embedded in tribal culture nor be a mystic to sense that the earth is wounded, that the life-support systems created over 4.5 billion years are endangered. There is a growing collective sense of "unprecedented pathology."[9] We are feeling a collective sense of earth's pain and realizing that we humans are responsible for inflicting much of that pain. Near the midpoint of our century, ecologist Aldo Leopold spoke of the "wounds of the world."[10] This sense of the earth's suffering has grown significantly *over the last fifty years*.

In the 1940s, the mushroom cloud provided a stark reminder that humankind had entered the atomic age. Human beings could send the planet into acute illness; a humanly-induced heart attack could befall the earth. We could annihilate the conditions for life, which took billions of years to achieve.

But human-induced illness to the planet can be *chronic* as well as *acute*. From the perspective of one in the United States, here are some markers of that realization.

In the 1950s, Rachel Carson and Jacques Cousteau, among others, called attention to the poisoning of the oceans.[11]

In the 1960s, pesticides and population were key themes.[12]

In the 1970s, nonrenewable resources and toxic waste showed us the input and final output of our consumer economy. E. F. Schumacher's 1973 *Small is Beautiful* called for changing our view of technological and economic life. Arne Naess elaborated the distinction between shallow and deep ecology. Barry Commoner and the Ehrlichs brought ecology and ecoscience to a widening audience.[13]

In the 1980s, problems of ozone and acid rain, the greenhouse effect, the rain forests and the extinction of species clearly underlined what was evident from outer space. National borders are neither markings on the earth nor barriers to contain atmospheric damage. In 1982, the United Nations approved the World Charter for Nature. The global nature of earth's illness was brought home to me in spring of 1988. At the top of one of China's holy mountains, Mount Emei in interior Sichuan province, I noticed that the dead trees showed the same signs of pollution as those I had seen on the top of Mount Mitchell in my home state of North Carolina. The air and waters circle the globe. That we are interconnected is now evident to our senses.[14]

I sum up the witness of pain to the planet by quoting Thomas Berry:

> In our times, . . . human cunning has mastered the deep mysteries of the earth at a level far beyond the capacities of earlier peoples. We can break the mountains apart; we can drain the rivers and flood the valleys. We can turn the most luxuriant forests into throwaway paper products. We can tear apart the great grass cover of the western plains and pour toxic chemicals into the soil and pesticides onto the fields until the soil is dead and blows away in the wind. We can pollute the air with acids, the rivers with sewage, the seas with oil — all this in a kind of intoxication with our power for devastation at an order of magnitude beyond all reckoning. We can invent computers capable of processing ten million calculations per second. *And why? To increase the volume and the speed with which we move natural resources through the consumer economy to the junk pile or the waste heap.*[15]

2. One Difficulty of Loving the Earth: Human Superiority

We are a part of this 4.5 billion years of earth's evolving. Some of us will see the need to preserve the earth so that there will be a world for our children. This view of responsible stewardship, while still human-centered, is a beginning. Deep Ecology takes the matter another step, emphasizing

(a) that, in our large self, we are the earth —
(large-Self realization) and
(b) that all beings have intrinsic worth (biocentric equality).[16]

Deep Ecology provides a perspective in which the two poles — preserving the earth for the sake of other species and for the sake of our own species — intertwine. They are, as the Buddhists might say, "not two, not one." Put differently, the other creatures are our elders; they are part of the conditions that sustain us; they are in us.

Yet we humans are still very young. We find it difficult to identify with our wider self as family, as nation, as humankind. How much more difficult to think beyond the human-centered, to break through to a planetary consciousness. Our biases are uncovered when we look at racism, sexism and speciesism.

We humans find it difficult to overcome *racism* (a *system* of racial discrimination that has its roots in one race having deep feelings of *superiority* over another and that is *sustained* by the institutions of the culture).

We humans find it difficult to overcome *sexism* (a *system* of sexual discrimination that has its roots in one sex having deep feelings of *superiority* over another and that is *sustained* by the institutions of the culture).

Will we not also find it difficult to overcome *speciesism* (a *system* of species discrimination which has its roots in one species (the human one) having deep feelings of *superiority* over other species and that is sustained by the institutions of the culture)?[17]

I emphasize the *systemic* nature of these "isms," their deep base in generalized feelings of *superiority*, and the fact that they are *sustained* by the institutions of the culture. The lesson is sobering. For sustainable change to take place in the planetary domain, correlative change is needed in the cultural and institutional domains as well as in the personal and familial domains.[18]

3. The Possibility of Loving the Earth:
Opportunities Old and New

Hopeful signs exist. We are recovering a planetary (and indeed cosmic) context for life. Theologian Matthew Fox, among others, has revived a creation-centered spirituality; physicist Brian Swimme echoes the quest for a new story in which spirituality, science and art, all have place.[19]

First, an experiential, poetic spirituality is a resource. More than an attitude, such a spirituality includes a practice — a way of life — that is liberative, appreciative, evocative and transformative. In the Confucian tradition, one speaks of a self-cultivation that returns us to the roots. For me, what funds the spiritual (depth dimension, sense of mystery) is the experience of the mystics (sages) and one's own experience in following the Way. Since the mystic tradition can be found within all cultural epochs and major cultures, the spiritual is not frozen into any one articulation.[20] We learn from the unity and diversity, from earth as spiritual guide.

Second, a nonreductionist, poetic science is a resource. Surely, the technological age makes it ever more clear that we share one world, one life support system, one web of economic interrelationship. Science itself is affirming interdependence.

Consider the following modification of Barry Commoner's principles of ecology:

1. Everything is interrelated.
2. Everything comes from somewhere.
3. Everything goes somewhere.
4. Nature knows best.[21]

Nature wastes little; what is cast off by one creature nourishes another. In a bioregion, species mutually limit one another. Self-sustaining cycles are everywhere in evidence. We can learn from earth as scientist, inventor, engineer par excellence. We can learn how to become cocreators of self-sustaining systems. Already, at its frontiers, science and poetry meet and both exhibit a profound respect for earth as weaver of life.

Third, an art open to the depth of life is a resource. We are beings on the earth, arising from the earth: we are also a mode of the earth's being.[22] Perhaps it is our destiny to give a particular voice to earth's beauty, as creators of symbol and story, poems of praise, and songs of wonder.[23] In the Taoist tradition, the return to nature is spoken in poetic voice. As Tom Early's translation of the *Tao Te Ching* has it:

> And see
> Now all things rise
> To flourish and return,
> Each creature coming
> To recover its roots.
>
> Recovering the root
> Means just this:
> The Dynamics of peace —
> Being recalled to our common fate
> In the kinship of all creation.[24]

The earth as a whole causes many to experience a depth in life and celebrate a mystery both vast and simple. Areas in particular bioregions are experienced as sacred places where initiation, healing, contemplation, and joyous identification occur. We become familiar with the earth as a whole by coming to love particular regions. As in works of art, the whole can be felt in the particular.

Thus, the paths of the sage, scientist and artist begin to converge; the practical and the poetic join as we realize interconnection, remain open to wonder, investigate life as it arises between the heavens and the earth, and learn from nature what it takes for self-sustaining harmony.

Every being proclaims a truth, embodies a worth, expresses a beauty. As a mode of earth's being, we humans (perhaps along with our brothers and sisters the whales and dolphins) seem to be earth's experiment with a type of self-reflective consciousness. We have the capacity to affirm in science the truths we discover and validate. We have the capacity to reverence in our spirituality the worth of all beings. We have the capacity as artists all to celebrate the beauty of life in song and story, myth and ritual, dance and design. Through us, earth finds a way for life to come to life through understanding, respect and celebration.

One of the four Confucian classics — the *Chung Yung* (*Doctrine of the Mean*) — goes beyond a human-centered focus to exhibit how humans can grow to become mirrors and partners with the great pattern of nature.

> Only those who are absolutely *sincere* (*ch'eng* - authentic, true)
>   can fully develop *their nature*.
> If they can fully develop their nature,
>   they can fully develop *the nature of others*.
> If they can fully develop the nature of others,
>   they can fully develop *the nature of things*.
> If they can fully develop the nature of things,
>   they can then assist in
>   *the transforming and nourishing processes*
>   *of Heaven and Earth*.
> If they can assist in the transforming and nourishing processes
>   of Heaven and Earth, they can then form
>   *a trinity with Heaven and Earth*.[25]

Here is the essence — the function of heaven and earth is "to bring into existence."[26] This function is evidenced in the realized person — the sage in us. In such moments, we form the "creative third" needed to assist in the transforming and nourishing processes of heaven and earth — the processes of coming to life more fully so as to serve life more wisely and more nobly.

Notes

1 Quoted in Thomas Berry, *The Dream of the Earth*, pp.14-15.

2 The universe itself could be considered a domain, since its context and temporal unfolding can be specified. Also, between earth as a domain and the universe as a domain, there lie, no doubt, other domains, perhaps of a galactic nature. However, we do not yet inhabit such space/time and I wish to keep the notion of domains rooted in the practical and experiential. Earth as a domain seems to be the widest material context/process of which we have growing experiential awareness.

3 Here I modify Thomas Berry's notion of epochs by moving from four to six such epochs. Using six epochs is sufficient and satisfactory for my purposes and matches the number of the domains. Of course, more epochs, like chapters in a story, can and must be specified for other purposes.

4 See Lovelock, *Gaia*, p. 11.

5 See Berry, *The Dream of the Earth*, p. 107.

6 *Ibid.*

7 See, for example, Riane Eisler, *The Chalice and the Blade*.

8 The reference is a less theistic way of rendering the Great Commandments of Deuteronomy 6:5. See also Matthew 22:37, Mark 12:30 and Luke 10:27.

9 The phrase is that of Thomas Berry in *The Dream of the Earth*.

10 See Aldo Leopold, *Sand County Almanac* (New York: Oxford, 1968; 1st pub. 1949).

11 See Rachael Carson, *The Sea Around Us* (New York: New American Library, 1961; 1st pub. 1951); see also Jacques Yves Cousteau *The Silent World* with Frederic Dumas (New York: Harper and Row, 1953) and *The Living Sea* with James Dugan (New York: Harper and Row, 1963).

¹² Rachel Carson's 1962 book, *Silent Spring*, is often cited as the beginning of the new wave of ecological thinking. The following year, Stewart Udall's *The Quiet Crisis* appeared. Later in the decade, the Club of Rome's Report brought population issues to the fore. See Rachel Carson, *Silent Spring* (Cambridge, MA: Riverside Press, 1962); Stewart L. Udall, *The Quiet Crisis* (New York: Holt, Rinehart and Winston, 1963); Donella H. Meadows et al., *The Limits to Growth* (New York: Universe Books, 1972) — a report for the Club of Rome's project on the predicament of mankind.

¹³ For E. F. Schumacher, see his *Small is Beautiful: Economics as if People Mattered* (New York: Harper and Row, 1973). For Arne Naess, see his *Ecology, Community and Lifestyle,* translated and edited by David Rothenberg (Cambridge: Cambridge University Press, 1989); see also Bill Devall and George Sessions, *Deep Ecology: Living as if Nature Mattered* (Salt Lake City: Peregrine Smith Books, 1985). Also note Barry Commoner, *The Closing Circle: Nature, Man and Technology* (New York: Alfred A. Knopf, 1971) and Paul R. Ehrlich, Anne H. Ehrlich and John P. Holdren, *Ecoscience: Population, Resources, Environment* (San Francisco: Freeman, 1977) as well as Paul and Anne Ehrlich, *Extinction: The Causes and Consequences of the Disappearance of Species* (San Francisco: Random House, 1981).

¹⁴ For a global overview, see State of the World reports published by Worldwatch Institute, Washington, D. C.

¹⁵ See Berry, *The Dream of the Earth,* p. 7. Italics mine.

¹⁶ See Bill Devall and George Sessions, *Deep Ecology*, chapter five.

¹⁷ For the definitions of racism, sexism and speciesism, I modify a scheme that I first learned from Hal Sieber when doing interracial workshops for the Greensboro Chamber of Commerce in the early 1970s.

¹⁸ Deep ecology is not without its critics, in large part because interdomain linkages are not made sufficiently explicit. For some of the debate, see Kirkpatrick Sales, "Deep Ecology and Its Critics," *The Nation*, May 14, 1988, pp. 670-75. I comment briefly on deep ecology and the Green Movement in the next chapter.

¹⁹ See Matthew Fox, *Original Blessing: A Primer in Creation Spirituality* (Sante Fe, NM: Bear and Company, 1983); see Brian Swimme, *The Universe is a Green Dragon*.

²⁰ Arne Naess uses this methodologically. See Bill Devall, *Simple in Means, Rich in Ends: Practicing Deep Ecology* (Salt Lake City: Peregrine Smith Books, 1988), p. 13.

[21] See Barry Commoner, *The Closing Circle*. Commoner's formulation is: (1) Everything is connected to everything else. (2) Everything must go somewhere. (3) Nature knows best. (4) There is no such thing as a free lunch; or, everything has to go somewhere.

[22] Berry makes the point often. See, e.g. *The Dream of the Earth*, p. 16. Arne Naess' attention to Spinoza also underscores the distinction.

[23] See Berry, *ibid.*, and Swimme, *The Universe*, for this theme.

[24] This passage is quoted in *Deep Ecology*, p. 14. The translation is beautiful; the terminology "creatures" and "all creation" are, however, misleading. Properly speaking, the Tao is not a creator.

[25] *Chung Yung*, XXII. See Wing-Tsit Chan, *A Source Book in Chinese Philosophy* (Princeton, NJ: Princeton University Press, 1963), pp. 107-08. Italics mine. For commentary, see Tu Wei-Ming, *Centrality and Commonality* (Albany, NY: State University of New York Press, 1989) — revised and enlarged edition.

[26] The phrase "the bringing into existence" is from the *I Ching*, Appendix III. It is quoted in Thomas Berry, "Affectivity in Classical Confucian Tradition," in *Riverdale Papers on China*.

CHAPTER NINE

THE CULTURAL DOMAIN: MYTHS AND RITUALS OF LIFE

Ch'en Kang asked [Confucius' son] Po-yü, "Have you not been taught anything out of the ordinary?"

"No, I have not. Once my father was standing by himself. As I crossed the courtyard with quickened steps [i.e. respectfully], he said, 'Have you studied the *Odes*?'

"I answered, 'No.'

"'Unless you study the *Odes*, you will be *ill-equipped to speak*.'

"I retired and studied the *Odes*.

"Another day, my father was again standing by himself. As I crossed the courtyard with quickened steps, he said, 'Have you studied the *Rites*?'

"I answered, 'No.'

"'Unless you study the *Rites*, you will be *ill-equipped to take your stand*.'

"I retired and studied the *Rites*. I have been taught these two things."

Ch'en Kang retired delighted and said, "I asked one question and got three answers. I learned about the *Odes*, I learned about the *Rites,* and I learned that a gentleman keeps aloof from his son."

— *Analects*, XVI:13 [1]

Confucius saw himself as training wise and effective leaders. If his own son was to be such a large-minded leader, then his education would be the same as that of any other student. Where did that education begin? With two classics: the *Book of Odes* and the *Book of Rites*.[2] For what purposes? So that, through the odes, the student would be well equipped *to speak* and, through the rites, the student would be well-equipped *to take a stand*.

To modern ears, this seems most strange. "What," we might ask, "have songs and rituals to do with leadership?" As a partial answer, I would offer the following:

The songs have to do with heritage. Think of a people's songs, stories and sayings; think of their folktales, fairytales and myths.[3] Surely, such rich metaphoric resources would allow one to speak in a way that touched the heart.

The rituals have to do with enactment. For example, myths are enacted in rituals; rituals are understood through the myths they make present. Think of the dances and ceremonies of native peoples; think of the intricate dance of diplomacy. Here one must know the dance to take one's stand; one must know the dance to bring a community to life in partnership with others.

The English word "culture" contains within it the word "cult." Cult points to song and dance, to ritual and mythic story. These lie at the heart of culture, where the artistic and religious intertwine.

A. THE CULTURAL DOMAIN IN ITS TIMESPAN

Culture can be seen as the shared set of meanings and values that inform the common way of life of a people.[4] Again, culture can be seen as the shared stories and symbols, myths and rituals that establish a people's sense of reality.[5]

For simplicity, suppose we link a culture to a people. I shall consider nations as cultures, without raising the issues of subcultures within a nation. Even as we become more globally aware, nations remain significant and nationalism remains a potent force for good and for ill. And yet diverse nations exist within certain deep structures, that I call cultural epochs. A national culture will stand in an epoch; the present cultural epoch will structure its dominant dreams.

In its widest reach, the cultural domain extends to the story of humankind. For the chapters in the human story, I shall make use of Thomas Berry's five cultural epochs. (See below.)

As the story of earth was a part of the larger story of the cosmos, so *the story of a cultural epoch is embedded in the story of the human race.* The five cultural epochs are presented sequentially; however, elements of earlier epochs can and do coexist with elements of later epochs. Indeed, we carry in us traces of all the epochs that have formed us.

Five Cultural Epochs:[6]
1. The matricentric epoch (Paleolithic and Neolithic) — worship of the Great Mother.
2. The patricentric, tribal epoch — often patriarchal, organizationally; shamanistic, religiously.
3. The epoch of the great classical religions and philosophies: the Egyptian, Babylonian, Persian, and Greek achievements; the religions of the Book (Judaism, Christianity, Islam); the Asian ways such as Buddhism, Confucianism and Taoism; the classical civilizations of the Mayans, Incas, Aztecs.
4. The modern (post 1500 A.D.) scientific, technological, industrial epoch.
5. The emerging ecological epoch.

Where are we in cultural time? We inhabit the modern period— between the classical epoch and the emerging ecological epoch.

CLASSICAL   MODERN   EMERGING ECOLOGICAL

Whether we accept or reject religion, many of us take our *notion* of religion from the classical epoch; our science and technology from the modern epoch; and our newest hope from the emerging ecological epoch.

In the last chapter, I noted the difficulties of transcending human-centeredness. Let us briefly look at the roots of this human-centeredness through several epochs:

1. The Classical Epoch: Higher Is Better

In Christianity of the classical epoch, the earth was below; God, above. Between earth and God stretched — ladder-like — the Great Chain of Being from rocks and minerals at the bottom rung, through plants, animals, humans, angels, and thence to God at the highest rung. (See chart for greater detail.)

THE GREAT CHAIN OF BEING:
MEDIEVAL CHRISTIAN VERSION

GOD
THE IMMATERIAL UNCREATED CREATOR

Angels
(immaterial but created lifeforms)

Humans

In the Public Sphere

Lords Spiritual (Church)	Lords Temporal (Kingdoms)
Pope Bishops Priests Laypeople	King Greater Nobles Lesser Nobles Peasants

In the Home

The Husband
The Wife
The Children

Animals

Plants

Minerals/Elements[7]

Throughout, *higher was better*. Higher was also more immaterial; lower, more densely material. Non-material was good; material was (*pace* God himself in Genesis) bad.

Nor is this the worst of it. Take a three-storied universe — heaven-earth-hell. Add a Manichee-type scheme that posits two gods — a Good God of Light and a Bad God of Darkness. Or, equivalently, conceive of life as a great battle between God of the Heavens and Satan from Hell on the battlefield of earth. This is a recipe for dualism with a vengeance. When earth and matter and flesh are claimed by evil, then heaven and spirit and soul are alone what is good. The world is dualistically divided. Those who sing Gospel do not sing the Blues.

In Dante's *Divine Comedy*, the three-headed Satan is polar opposite of the Trinity. The Trinity, like the sun, represents life and light and warmth; Satan inhabits the center of the earth in a realm of death, darkness and ice. The earth belongs to darkness and devils. No wonder that it is seen at the periphery of creation.

2. *The Modern Epoch: Later Is Better*

The Great Chain of Being was vertical, static and eternal; the nineteenth century picture of evolution was horizontal (linear), developmental and firmly in time. "Earlier vs. later" replaced "lower vs. higher." From matter came simple plant life, then animal life and then human life.

The good news, we might now say, was (a) the notion of development itself,[8] and (b) the realization of our interconnection with all other lifeforms.[9]

The bad news, we might now say, was that one assumption remained. "Higher is better" survived as "later is better." Anthropocentrism survived. The century of Darwin was also a century of high imperialism.

3. *The Emerging Ecological Epoch: Biocentric Is Better*

The journey of the astronauts from earth toward the stars — occurring a century after Darwin — is more modest than Dante's journey in *The Divine Comedy*. The astronauts went only to the moon. And yet the result of this experience was quite different from Dante's. The earth was not relegated to the periphery nor was material creation degraded. Instead, the earth became center again, in a new and powerful sense. We are coming to see our planet in its wholeness and to love it deeply as home. While the Apollo 11 Mission was speeding away from earth at nearly 25,000 miles per hour, astronaut Collins reflected: "I am conscious of distance. Distance *away from home*. It is a sobering, almost melancholy, sight, this shrinking globe. . . ."[10]

Two crucial differences mark the transition from the evolutionary story, at least as culturally told, to the story of emergence.

First, we must finally let go of the human superiority that haunted both the Great Chain (higher is better) and the commonly understood story of evolution (later is better). We must move from anthropocentrism to bio- or eco-centrism.

Second, in the commonly told evolution story, earth is the setting of evolution; in domain six and in deep ecology, earth is itself the evolving subject.

Devall and Sessions provide a contrast between the dominant worldview of the modern epoch and what we call (with Berry) the emerging ecological epoch. The Devall and Sessions comparison is as follows:[11]

DOMINANT WORLDVIEW	DEEP ECOLOGY
Dominance over Nature	Harmony with Nature
Natural environment as resource for humans	All nature has intrinsic worth/biospecies equality
Material/economic growth for growing human population	Elegantly simple material needs (material goals serving the larger goal of self-realization)
Belief in ample resource reserves	Earth "supplies" limited
High technological progress and solutions	Appropriate technology; nondominating science
Consumerism	Doing with enough/recycling
National/centralized community	Minority tradition/bioregion

Deep Ecology is here representing an emerging ecological awareness. An analogous picture (though more centered on the political level) is drawn by the Green Movement with their four pillars: ecology, social responsibility, grassroots democracy and nonviolence.[12]

When one compares epochs, certain cultural assumptions may be brought to light and examined.

B. The Cultural Domain in Its Community Aspect

The planetary domain is a community of all beings of the earth in the time of aeons. The cultural domain is a community of all human beings whose story has unfolded in the time of millennia. In every epoch, we see humans in organized groups —tribes, kingdoms, empires, nations, etc. All of humankind, socially organized, presents itself as a community of communities. Today, humans are mainly to be found in nation-states. The United Nations, while not an effective world federation, gives a glimpse of what such a community of communities might be like.

Where are we of the United States in the cultural domain? We exist in a nation within a community of nations. Our nation's institutions gain their meaning and value from the cultural epoch in which they stand. The cultural epoch is part of the human story. The human race is one species in the wider community of all earth's creatures.

Thus, in the cultural domain we are clearly within interwoven domains. We stand within the nation (institutional domain) conscious of the story of humankind (cultural domain) in the wider context of all living beings (planetary domain).

Planetary — All Living Beings

Cultural — Humankind
(Classical — Modern — Emerging Ecological)

Institutional — The Nation

C. Culture and the Genius of Confucius

Confucius lived at a time of warring feudal states; his concern was to create a common culture — a culture that would be constantly and authentically recreated using the old as resources for the new.[13] As Confucius put it: "The one who by reanimating the old gains knowledge of the new is indeed worthy to be called teacher." (*Analects* 2:11)

Herbert Fingarette, in a seminal work, *Confucius — The Secular as Sacred*, writes:

> Two great insights fused in Confucius' thought. Confucius, the political man, conceived that the social crisis required *cultural unity* as an essential ground of *political-social unity*. And Confucius, the philosophical anthropologist, affirmed *life lived in the image of the authentic ceremonial act* as the necessary and

sufficient condition of *authentic humanity*. The implications of these themes taken jointly call for political-social unity to be ceremonial. And this in turn calls for a tradition-oriented culture as essential ground out of which ceremony is nourished.[14]

Confucius appeals to neither coercive leadership nor solitary asceticism. Rather he teaches nobility, service and humane living, all in the context of community. In this, he draws on the deepest springs of humanity: friendship, family and kingdom. In Confucius' view, as Fingarette notes, "to become civilized is to establish relationships that are not merely physical, biological or instinctive; it is to establish *human* relationships, relationships of an essentially symbolic kind, defined by tradition and convention and rooted in respect and obligation."[15]

Thus, we see Confucius pointing to the great Sage-kings of old — whose gifts were the founding of culture, and to the more recent King Wen and King Wu and the Duke of Chou — whose gifts were wise and effective rule. We see the Confucian school in the forefront of recovering the Five Classics — especially the *Book of Odes*, the *Book of Rituals*, the *Books of History*, and that great work that synthesizes all domains —the *Book of Changes*. We can now begin to grasp more fully the story told at the start of this chapter. Here, Confucius tells his son that without grounding in poetic language (the *Book of Odes*), he will not be able to speak wisely, diplomatically and effectively. He tells his son that, without skill in the ceremonies of life (the *Book of Rituals*), he will not be able to take a stand.

Before prose, there is poetry. Before science, art. Before becoming separate, we are held in relationship. Before being explained, life is evoked in singing and dancing, story and ceremony. All of this is not for itself, but for creating, recreating, and sustaining "a compassionate heart."[16]

The cultural domain centers on the power of myth and ritual. Myth in its most positive sense is a story that points to mystery, that evokes what we find most meaningful and valuable, that speaks heart to heart. Ritual provides an acting out of myth; myth provides the significance of ritual. Usually, myth and ritual are presented as mirroring the realm of gods and spirits. For Confucius, ritual calls us to actualize the human. It is grounded firmly in the human story.[17]

The rituals evoke *primal symbols*: the earth and heavens, the sun and moon, the lake and the mountains, the parent and child, ruler and kingdom. The rituals evoke *primal events*: marriage and family, the birth of children, teaching and learning, service at home and in the world, aging and dying. This is the human way and everyone follows it to some extent. Yet Confucius calls his students to be in the world in a noble, courteous manner, to participate in the events of life consciously, compassionately and continuously.

Confucius redefined nobility to make it a matter not of birth but of achievement — accessible to all. Such nobility does have its obligations ("noblesse oblige") — obligations to enter public service, to act for the welfare of the community. As one of his students said: "The Master is good at leading one on step by step. He broadens me with culture and brings me back to the essentials by means of the rites."[18] The essentials deal with life in relationship — especially the five relationships.[19] And yet one must see these relationships in the social-political sphere, under a cultural story, within the cosmos itself.[20]

According to Confucius, we become human in a human community sharing a culture and tradition, living out the relationships of institutional, family and friendship domains. In these domains, we begin with the four key virtues (or four beginnings):

jen — *benevolence or human-heartedness,*
yi — *a justice-like sense of appropriateness,*
li — *a taste and skill in ritual and*
chih — *a practical wisdom in noble living.*

These virtues are "the four beginnings" of becoming human (humane). A passage from Mencius will give a flavor of the four virtues:

What is the foundation of natural human feeling for others (*jen*)? The heart that sympathizes with pain. What is the foundation of a commitment to the common good (*yi*)? The heart that's repelled by vice. What is the foundation of respect for social and religious forms (*li*)? The heart that's willing to defer. And what is the foundation of a liberal education (*chih*)? The heart that can tell true from false. *Mencius* II, A, 6. [21]

Confucius is indeed a master of the fifth domain — understanding the realm of meaning and value, story and symbol, and utilizing the power of tradition to build community with a human (humane) face.

D. Culture and Language:
What Is Revealed and Concealed

Early in this chapter, I introduced Lonergan's shorthand definition of culture as a set of meanings and values that informs a common way of life. This definition can be fleshed out by seeing the set of meanings and values as a set of common or complementary *experiences, understandings, convictions* and *commitments*. This allows us to point out the following:

Besides attention to experience, there is inattention and avoidance. Besides insight and understanding, there is oversight and misunderstanding. Beside modest, wise judgment, there is prejudice and partial judgment. Beside commitment to lasting values and vital needs, there is the lure of the superficial and the shoddy, the faddish and unnecessary, the self-serving and destructive. Cultures may be healthy or sick, self-correcting or self-deluding, in development or in decline. Truth to tell, all cultures include signs of both. They see and are blind, reveal and conceal, support and undermine quality.

Culture's contribution is to provide a framework of shared meaning and value for a people; its entry point is language, broadly considered to include all forms of the symbolic. We internalize the cultural paradigm as we learn to speak and dream in the culture's words and images.

The language and symbolism of a culture are a powerful ally of both exploitation and liberation. When groups challenge a culture's assumptions, they often do so by calling for a change in language. In the United States, the black movement has challenged white superiority; the women's movement has challenged male superiority; the deep ecology movement has challenged human superiority. All have sought to change ways of thinking and acting, in part, by changing ways of speaking.

The language and symbolism of a culture are also powerful resources for action and change. Consider Elizabeth Cady Stanton and Lucretia Mott's 1864 "Declaration of Sentiments" and Martin Luther King's "I Have a Dream" speech. Think of Elizabeth the First mobilizing her nation against Spain and Winston Churchill's World War II speech to the nation. Recall Golda Meir and Franklin Delano Roosevelt calling their nations to sacrifice. But also consider Torquemada and the Inquisition, Hitler and the Nuremburg rally, McCarthyism in the postwar United States, Mao Tse Tung's *Little Red Book* in the Chinese Cultural Revolution, and the Ayatollah Khomeini's influence in Iran. As

Ernest Becker shows in his treatment of "transference heroics" and scapegoating, humans as symbolic animals can be led to the heights and the depth through myth and metaphor.[22]

Gibson Winter states that "... the human species dwells symbolically on the earth."[23] Confucius bids us be aware of this and he asks us to go to the roots of human culture. Going to the roots is an exercise in recovering what it means to be human. Confucius examined one culture and exhibited the humane qualities at its roots. Today, we are more aware of the plurality of cultures both in space and in time. For us, to be faithful to Confucius' project is to go beyond it. Indeed, the challenge of the cultural domain requires of us the following:

> to expand the cultural domain from our epoch to the entire story of humankind,
> to bring to life the criteria of the human,
> to honor those exemplars who have established and extended the human,
> to be on guard against those which have, on balance, degraded life and cosmos.

In our time, the cultural work must be *critical* (to uncover oppression) and *creative* (to bring to life more fully).

The earth domain invites us to revive a larger vision of the planet and its bioregions. It invites us to create a cosmic story wherein spirituality, science and art can dwell together.[24]

The cultural domain invites us to rediscover what it means to be human across cultures and across epochs. This domain invites us to a larger vision of humankind, our cultural epochs, and the communities that tend the cultural treasures. It invites us to rediscover the wisdom of the Great Mother and the shamanic vision of the native peoples, to go to the roots of the mystic traditions of the historic religions and the perennial philosophy, to recover the perception of mystery of the great scientists. To go to the roots of these traditions and to recover authentic criteria for human life and living — this is the challenge of the emerging ecological age.

The cultural domain — the domain of how we speak and dream collectively — places us in contact with the human story and, even more deeply, calls us to understand what is truly human, humane, life-enhancing and what is not. We come to life more fully in the cultural domain when we prize the unity of human experience and the diversity of its expression, when we creatively enact shareable cross-cultural and cross-epochal criteria for human living. Such standards of the human and humane incorporate what our wisest and noblest humans have discovered; such standards are open to insights from our nonhuman elders in the earth domain and can provide guidance for our life in the institutional domain.

Notes

1. See Confucius, *The Analects* (Lun Yü), trans. D.C. Lau (New York: Viking Penguin, 1979). Italics mine.

2. See chapter two of this work for background.

3. The poet Robert Bly distinguishes folktales, fairytales and myths along the following lines: In folktales, the characters are ordinary people. In fairytales, there is the presence not only of characters from this world, but also characters from another world; but the characters from the other world are in disguise, as it were, and we do not know their real names. In myths, the gods appear in their own names. Bly made these distinctions in a public poetry reading at Meredith College, Raleigh, NC, in the spring of 1988.

4. The core of this definition — that culture is a set of meanings and values that inform a common way of life — I take from Bernard Lonergan. See Lonergan, *Method in Theology* (New York: Herder and Herder, 1972).

5. For an early but still excellent introduction to the narrative nature of culture, see Michael Novak's *Ascent of the Mountain, Flight of the Dove* (New York: Harper and Row, 1971).

6. For the five cultural epochs or phases, see Berry, *The Dream of the Earth*, pp. 93 and 101-05; also chapters five and eleven. The particular formulation in this chart is mine.

7. For the first four ranks, see the scheme that E. F. Schumacher uses to symbolize the Great Chain of Being: m = matter; add to matter "life" (x) and we get m + x = plant life; add to material lifeforms "consciousness" (y) and we get m+x+y = conscious animal life; add to conscious material lifeforms "a capacity for higher consciousness" (z) and we get m+x+y+z = human life. See Schumacher, *A Guide for the Perplexed* (New York: Harper and Row, 1977).

8. Hegel, Marx, Darwin, Freud, and Piaget are all, in one sense or another, developmentalists. For a flavor of this impact, see Robert Kegan, *The*

Evolving Self, and Ken Wilber, *Up From Eden: A Transpersonal View of Human Evolution* (Boulder, CO: Shambhala Publications, 1981).

[9] As Timothy Ferris remarks: "Darwinian evolution, in indicating that all species of earthly life are related and that all arose from ordinary matter, made it clear that there is no wall dividing us from our fellow creatures on earth, or from the planet that gave us all life — that we are such stuff as worlds are made of." See Timothy Ferris, *Coming of Age in the Milky Way* (New York: Doubleday, 1988), pp. 367-68.

[10] See Timothy Ferris, *Spaceshots: The Beauty of Nature Beyond Earth* (New York: Pantheon Books, 1984), p.141.

[11] Taken from Devall and Sessions, *Deep Ecology*, p. 69.

[12] See Fritjof Capra and Charlene Spretnak, *Green Politics* (New York: Dutton, 1984, p.125. For evidence that Green Politics also covers other domains, see Charlene Spretnak, *The Spiritual Dimension of Green Politics* (Sante Fe, NM: Bear and Company, 1986). I would say that, in addition to hierarchy/equality, other imbalances needing reframing and redress are: control over nurturance, individualism over community, the analytic over the poetic, and the tendency to think in terms of static "things" rather than interrelated processes.

[13] For a look at Confucius that emphasizes this process aspect of culture, see Hall and Ames, *Thinking Through Confucius*.

[14] See Herbert Fingarette, *Confucius — The Secular as Sacred* (New York: Harper and Row, 1972), p. 64. Italics mine.

[15] *Ibid.*, p. 76.

[16] The phrase "the compassionate heart" is from Mencius. See *Mencius*, trans. D.C. Lau (New York: Penguin Books, 1970), Book 2A:6

[17] See *Analects* XI:12.

[18] *Analects* IX:11.

[19] The five relationships — ruler-minister; parent-child; husband-wife; elder-younger; and friend-friend — are discussed in chapter eleven on the family domain. For the five relationships, see *Chung Yung* XX: 8; for the correlated functions, see *Mencius* III:4; for commentary, see Tu Wei-Ming, *Centrality and Commonality*, pp. 55-56.

[20] On Confucian "integral humanism," see Tu Wei-Ming's essay on Confucian religiousness in *Centrality and Commonality*. Tu Wei-Ming likewise speaks of Confucian teaching going beyond the ethical to the "anthropocosmic." The phrase is Mircea Eliade's — combining "anthropos" (man or human) and "cosmos"; it is appropriated by Tu Wei-Ming, *ibid.*, p. 9 and elsewhere.

Regarding this, Tu Wei-Ming writes: "[The] Confucian perception of the human as an anthropocosmic idea adds a transcendent dimension to Confucian ethics. Indeed, the anthropocosmic vision is so much an integral part of Confucian moral persuasion that, without an appreciation of the basic anthropocosmic (thus meta-ethical) principles, we cannot understand how Confucian ethics actually works." p. 102.

[21] Quoted from William McNaughton, ed., *The Confucian Vision* (Ann Arbor, MI: University of Michigan Press, 1974), p. 62. D.C. Lau translates as follows: the heart of compassion, the heart of shame, the heart of courtesy and modesty, and the heart of right and wrong.

See Lau, *Mencius*, 2 A:6. I alter the spelling *i* to *yi* for consistency.

[22] See Becker, *The Denial of Death*, as well as Ernest Becker, *Escape from Evil* (New York: Free Press, 1975) and *The Structure of Evil* (New York: Free Press, 1976). Also relevant is Sam Keen, *Faces of the Enemy: Reflections of the Hostile Imagination* (New York: Harper and Row, 1986).

[23] See Gibson Winter, *Liberating Creation* (New York: Crossroad Publishing, 1981), p. xiii. Winters speaks of founding symbols, root metaphors, praxis, and unconscious motivational symbols which open out to "archetypal rhythms of bios and cosmos." See pp. 26, 44, 66-70. All this resonates with the Confucian project.

[24] The voice of Matthew Fox echoes here.

CHAPTER TEN

THE INSTITUTIONAL DOMAIN: THE KINGDOM THAT IS WITHOUT

Hot springs, sumptuous feasts —
Such are for nobles only, not for common folk.
But the silks given away in token of imperial grace
Are from the looms of poor women
Whose husbands, thrashed into submission,
Had to offer their home products as tribute.
The emperor's bounty is intended to encourage
Loyal service to the country.
If this is not borne in mind,
Largesse becomes sheer waste.

— *the poet Tu Fu (written A.D. 755)[1]*

Imagine once again a stone tossed into still waters. Hear the small splash and watch the concentric ripples arise from the center and move outward.

Imagine that we are watching the ripples in an ornamental pond. We are in China in the early summer of A.D. 755, a fateful year almost at the midpoint of the Tang dynasty (A.D. 618-907). The pond is at the Huaqing Hot Springs near Mount Li, east of the old Chinese capital, Chang'an (modern Xi'an). Members of the court in their finery have joined the Emperor at his summer resort. One of their number has casually tossed the stone into the pond.

Next, imagine that this scene of courtiers langidly amusing themselves is seen through the eyes of the great poet, Tu Fu (Du Fu). Tu Fu's comments on such a scene appear in the poem that heads this chapter.

We have viewed the scene in three steps: First, the ripples on the still water lull us. Next, the courtiers idling about in richly embroidered clothes enchant our senses. Finally, we see, through the eyes of Tu Fu, the danger of wealth and power disconnected from service. "The emperor's bounty is intended to encourage loyal service to the country," he writes in the above poem. "If this is not borne in mind, largesse becomes sheer waste."

With Tu Fu's comment, we are suddenly in the political realm, the institutional domain, the circle that lies at the midpoint of the seven. Entering this domain, we see the powerful and the powerless, the very rich and the very poor, the just and the unjust, the compassionate and the cruel. All are here. At this moment of entering the fourth domain, something chilling occurs, as when clouds pass before the sun and a summer's day goes cold.

The institutional domain has, as its community aspect, the *network of institutions* within a national cultural framework; its time is the *age of those institutions* — usually measured in centuries. Consider what I shall call the Big Four Institutions — (i) political, (ii) economic, (iii) educational (including media) and (iv) religious. As examples, think of a branch of government, a corporation, a college, an organized religious body.

The world of institutions is close to us, impacting us in terms of our work and well-being, political power, access to knowledge, even our behavior and ideals. The arena of organized life is larger than us, older than us. The world of institutions is the space of structured life, the world of roles, rules and routines; power, policies and procedures. No wonder we may feel a chill to enter here.

A. HERE BE DRAGONS OF THE DEEP
Imagine that our ornamental pond transforms itself and becomes a great ocean connecting two mythic continents. The continent of the

West is called the Land of the Far Shore; the continent of the East is called the Land of the Near Shore. Legend says that there is an island in the middle of this ocean surrounded by fierce seas and great monsters. Each continent has its cartographers, though the map makers see the world from different points of origin. The Far Shore cartographers map from West to East; in the dangerous seas before the legendary island, they write: "Here be dragons!" The Near Shore cartographers map from East to West; they come from the other direction toward the unruly seas surrounding the island. And they too write: "Here be dragons!"

My allegory is of the domains pictured thus:

F A R						N E A R
	6	5	4	3	2	
	Planet	Cultural	Political	Family	Interpersonal	
S H O R E	all life	all human life	institutional life	family life	friendship life	S H O R E

To come from the left, from the far shore, is to come from the Tao expressed in its vastness. We next move to consider all life on the planet and then encounter the entire human story in five epochs. If we start from vastness, colored by myth and ritual, then what is unknown and fearful is the nonfictional, the "smaller than ideal" life. From this direction, the political realm appears to be *too small*. To the cosmic thinkers of the far shore, the political realm seems a snare of petty concerns and mixed motives.

To come from the right, from the near shore, is to come from the Tao expressed in intimate simplicity. We next move to the friendships of life and then move through generations of family, from grandparents to grandchildren. If we start from intimacy, then what is unknown and fearful are matters that are impersonal, the specter of a society of strangers, unbonded by friendship or family.[2] From this direction, the political realm appears to be *too large*. To the intimate thinker of the near shore, the political realm seems cold and calculating, abstract and unfeeling.

We may now grasp why journeyers into the waters of the institutional domain feel that monsters of the deep lurk here. Without courage, voyagers from both shores would turn back.

The fourth domain lies in the center of the seven. We can catch sight of its intermediate nature in yet a different way. If, for the moment, we treat the Tao and the planetary domains as one and the personal and interpersonal domains as one, we can place the body politic between the body planetary and the body personal as in the chart (opposite).

B. The General Nature of Institutions: A Modern Viewpoint

The fourth domain is the field of collaborative action — especially the action of the Big Four corporate players. To understand this domain, we must understand the nature of institutions — as solutions to a certain sort of task, as rule-and-role structures, and as the arenas of power, justice and social class.

1. Institutions as Solutions to a Certain Sort of Task

Some human needs recur. I need to eat today and will need to eat tomorrow. I cannot satisfy my hunger permanently. Furthermore, periodic hunger and the need for food is not peculiar to me alone; it is a recurrent need that affects all people. All people must devise ways to meet this recurrent need or perish. The problem that gives rise to institutions will be a recurrent one: e.g., ordering life and settling disputes, providing goods and services, educating the young.

The form of solution to such a problem will involve division of labor and cooperative action. Dividing up tasks makes sense. But divided labor, if it is to be effective, requires coordination. Thus, the practice of dividing and coordinating labor becomes a social arrangement and an institution is born.

Let us summarize: Institutions can be viewed as a response to human needs that (i) *recur* and (ii) *affect all or many people and (iii) require or benefit from cooperative actions*.

The stability of institutions over time is called for by the recurrent nature of the task. The cooperative aspect of institutions is called for by the benefits of division and coordination of labor.

Hence, we understand institutions as organized cooperative

The Planet Earth Domain
The Time of Cosmic Unfolding

Key Image: THE BODY PLANETARY

(Includes awareness of earth as the primary
self-governing, self-sustaining system)

Intermediary:
The Cultural Domain
The Time of Human Cultural Unfolding

(Includes awareness of the story of humankind
and exploration of the criteria for being human)

The Institutional (or Kingdom) Domain
The Time of the Nation

Key Image: THE BODY POLITIC or CORPORATE

(Includes emphasis on task and on service
in collaborative endeavors)

Intermediary:
The Family Domain
The Time of Generations

(Includes expansion of time without loss of personal uniqueness)

The Personal/Interpersonal Domain
from the Moment to the Lifetime

Key Image: THE BODY PERSONAL
and relationships between actual, flesh and blood others

(Includes first awareness of stillness, within; service, without)

structures, existing over time, to satisfy recurring human needs. Here, an example will clarify the matter.

Suppose that I must move from one house or apartment to another. I may ask friends and family members to give me a hand. We come together as a group, accomplish the task, celebrate and disperse. It is, for us, a "one-shot" affair. On the other hand, we could decide to become the Ace Moving Company in order to provide quality moving services for the many people who, at any given time, are moving. We might make a division of labor, appoint company officers, incorporate, set up rules and roles, institute policies and procedures, etc. We would then be an institution.

2. Roles, Rules and Routines in Service of the Task

Institutions such as governments, schools, corporations, etc. are not simply a grouping of people. Like the human body, institutions are organized systems; unlike the human body, these systems appear as *systems of roles, rules and routines.* The *roles* remain relatively fixed. Now this person, now another person, fills the roles. The *rules* are made, taught, and become relatively fixed. Finally, we say: "That's the way things are. You can't fight City Hall." The *routines* take place day in and day out. People get used to them and rely on them. The routines harden into habits, hard to break. The roles, rules and routines can be changed, but change is difficult; people resist; habits persist.

The sociologists, Berger and Luckmann, remind us that institutions are formed by people; time passes; and people become formed by the institutions.[3] The roles, rules and routines give a permanence to institutions. In large part, the key institutions are present before we are born and will go on after we die. Institutional time is a time larger than the lifetime, larger even than the time of generations. We dwell within an organized world and that world becomes a part of who we are and how we live.

Nonetheless, remembering that institutions arise to fulfill tasks is valuable. It allows us to hold two factors in mind: *Some form of basic institution is necessary* (because the problem will remain), while, at the same time, *any particular form of institution is somewhat arbitrary* (being only one possible solution to the problem).

This allows us to acknowledge institutions in their origin and intent, while avoiding an idolatry of the *status quo.*

There is yet another reason to keep tasks in view. With the task in view, we can see that sometimes the roles and rules and routines aid in accomplishing the task; sometimes, they become separated from the task, stuck in outdated routines, starved for vitality and creativity. Keeping the task in mind helps us to judge how well the current structure is meeting its goals.

3. Power, Policies and Procedures in Service of the Task

So far, we have looked at institutions as collaborative solutions to recurrent needs and as structures of roles, rules and routines already in place. Now, we introduce considerations of power and social class.

Institutional power is the power to make policies and procedures. Some hold institutional power; some do not. Social classes can be seen in this light. Those who make or influence governmental and business policy, who, through media and education, shape the nation's dream, determine a total system with power to reward and punish. Those with power speak via policies and procedures; those without power simply confront the policies and procedures as factors much like fate.

Because the institutional domain is the domain of power (through policies and procedures), it is also the preeminent domain for justice to enter in. "Justice," in one striking formulation, "is sorting out what belongs to whom and giving it back."[4] Both justice and injustice, liberation and exploitation, have their prime residence in this fourth domain, in the world of institutions. All justice, one might proclaim, is social justice. In this light, we begin to realize how much of what is called "the real world" is the institutionally structured world.

4. Three Problems in the Institutional Domain

Return now to my story of the fourth domain as an island surrounded by rough seas and powerful monsters.

Recall that those from the near shore, beginning with intimacy, fear the institutional domain for its impersonality and, now I might add, for its hierarchical power relationships. Those starting from intimacy — the domains of friendship and family — perceive institutions as too big.

Recall that those from the far shore, beginning with global vision and the diversity of cultures, fear the institutional domain for its self-enclosed concerns, its unwillingness to seek a higher good. Those starting from an international, global sense — the domains of planet and all humanity — perceive institutions as too small.

We can gather both sentiments under the heading of the following three problems that institutions have in our modern epoch:

First, the *impersonality* aspect of institutions (e.g. that the role is independent of the one holding the role) may be needed for continuity. Nonetheless, this "substitutability" feature seems to make particular individuals standardized, disposable, and unimportant. The uniqueness of individuals disappears.

Second, the *power* aspect of institutions (e.g. hierarchy of bosses and workers, those who make policy and those who follow policy) may be needed to coordinate the action in service of a task. Nonetheless, when power is seen as "power over," then a separation occurs between those who do (the doers) and those who are done to (the receivers). Next, only the "doers" are counted as part of the institution. Thus, we find it hard to see students as an integral part of educational institutions and patients as an integral part of medical institutions, hard to see citizens as an integral part of political institutions and customers as an integral part of economic institutions. Furthermore, as institutions become more bureaucratized, we start to think that only "real" doers are top management, that all other role holders are receivers. Disidentification and lack of felt collaborative "ownership" of the enterprise quickly follow.

Lastly, the *task* aspect of institutions can itself get lost as image replaces reality. Legislators may lose sight of legislative justice, of laws as furthering the common good — what is good for the whole and fair to each representative part. Judges and lawyers may lose sight of the task of judicial justice, of the wise and fair resolution of disputes. Educators may lose sight of teaching and learning; doctors may lose sight of healing. Those in business may lose sight of providing goods and services; those in religious ministries may lose sight of the great mystery, fail to foster spirituality, abandon the painful call to name injustice, and overlook cultivation of a compassionate heart.

C. The Network of the Kingdom from an Ancient Chinese Viewpoint

"The one who by rediscovering the old can contribute to the new is indeed worthy to be called a teacher."[5] Can the ancient Chinese approach to institution suggest ways to bring our institutions to life more fully? I believe they can, and in the following three ways:

1. A Different Sense of Order

In their work on Confucius, Hall and Ames distinguish between logical order and aesthetic order. In their view, "aesthetic order presses in the direction of particularity and uniqueness; logical order toward generality and absolute substitutability."[6]

In logical order, the pre-existing pattern is primary; what embodies the pattern, the particulars, the parts, is secondary. One can have the same pattern and different parts. To substitute one set of particulars for another does not affect the pattern. Clearly, when we think of institutions in a Western framework, we assume logical order; the institution becomes a set of roles and rules; any individual person is dispensable.

Aesthetic order, on the other hand, stresses particularity, uniqueness, performance. As in painting, the particulars matter; as in the performing arts, the performance of this playwright, these actors and this director interacting this way on this night before this audience matters. Time and particularity enter strongly.

Of course, the distinction is not an absolute one.[7] Substitution is possible *and* the performance is different.

The modern picture sees clearly that the roles must be independent of the occupant for the institution to go on. Seeing this, we stress substitutability. Confucius too realizes this, but tends toward aesthetic, open-ended order and welcomes the interaction between inheritance and personal contribution. Confucius sees political unity as resting on a shared heritage and acted out in awakened and awakening ritual action. If institutions are to be considered in this light, particularity and time will be stressed. Think of a football coach designing an offense to make best use of the talent available; think of a playwright writing with a particular repertory company in mind.

Let us try to open a space for thinking in a way different from our accustomed mode. What might this be like?

First, institutions, more aesthetically considered, would, I think, prize particular persons more. Each person would count as a key part of the institutional structure; in schools, students would count as much as administrators and faculty; in corporations, customers would count as much as executives and employees. In thinking of the institution, we would think of the network of particular people serving and served as together comprising the institutional reality. How we define institutions would change.

Second, institutions, more aesthetically considered, would prize time more. Each person who was ever a part of an institution would always be a part of the institution and its story. How we identify institutions would change.

Third, institutions, more aesthetically considered, would think of *place in the ritual defined by models of excellence*, rather than *roles defined by impersonal rules*. How we consider position would change.

2. A Different Sense of Power

Recall how Confucius redefined nobility, from a quality gained by birth to a quality gained by virtue. Recall how Confucius contrasted the "chün tzu" — superior or exemplary or profound person — with the "hsiao jen" — the small-minded person.

Some two hundred years after Confucius, his devoted follower, Mencius, saw how easily virtue could be pushed aside in favor of short-sighted efficiency (skill in service of wealth or power). Mencius redefined the notion of hegemon (*pa*) to suggest improper domination by force for the sake of small-minded goals.[8] He contrasted this with the true king (*wang*) who cultivated virtue in himself and others for the sake of maintaining a benevolent government.

The comparison is clear: *As the profound person (chün-tzu) is continuous with the true king (wang), so the small-minded person (hsiao jen) is continuous with the hegemon (pa).*

Under this ideal, power becomes the power to "grow people," the power of promoting authentic humanity (*jen*), skill in the rituals of life (*li*), creative action appropriate to oneself and the situation at hand (*yi*), and wise judgment concerning the movements of life (*chih*). The Chinese word *zhi* means to govern, to heal, and to prune back. The ideogram combines (i) a river flowing between banks and (ii) a mouth. Thus, to govern, heal, prune is to facilitate growth through appropriate limits and effective communication. Authority held by exemplars of service for the sake of the common good is quite different from power held by those who have captured roles for the sake of self or class interest.

3. A Different Sense of Task

Recall the twelve officials or functions. Recall a parallel between functions in body personal and functions in the body politic or corporate. These functions, simplified to four, are:

Sovereign of Awakened Heart
TASK

Strategic General   First Minister
TACTICS   TRANSMISSION

Master of Deep Waters
TREASURY/TRADITION

Can we make a correlation between the Big Four institutions and the four officials first introduced? Perhaps we can do so as a speculation. Consider the following arrangement:

Like the Compassionate Sovereign,

POLITICS
as creating conditions of
C.A.R.E. = collaborative
and respectful existence

Like the Strategic General,   Like the First Minister,

ECONOMICS   RELIGION
as protecting and   as encouraging
providing for the   the widest vision
people's well-being   to be embodied in life

Like the Minister of Deep Waters,

EDUCATION
as transmitting the heritage

What also becomes clear in this arrangement is that any institution can be looked on as having:
a political aspect of providing just, nourishing, and
     effective structuring,
a religious aspect of linking the heavens and the earth,
an educational aspect of continued learning and
     remembrance of heritage, and
an economic aspect of remaining viable in the world.[9]

All of this, in the Chinese classics, has as its aim the well-being of the people. Mencius underlines these points throughout. In speaking of the sage kings Yu and Chi, Mencius says: "Yu looked upon himself as responsible for anyone in the Empire who drowned; Chi looked upon himself as responsible for anyone in the Empire who starved."[10] And again, "It was through losing the people that [the tyrants] Chieh and Tchou lost the Empire, and through losing the people's hearts that they lost the people."[11] *Task, service*, and the *well-being of the people* remain central.

D. Coming to Life in the Institutional Domain

I opened this chapter with the image of courtiers at an ornamental pond, with the image of the poet Tu Fu reflecting on justice and the common good. Our focus has also been on holding a sense of *task*, as the sovereign of awakened heart holds the task for the kingdom.

Next, the pond changed to an ocean with the world of institutions as an island at the center. The fourth domain does indeed exist at the center of the full seven domains, at the center of the five intermediate domains:

F A R S H O R E	6	5	4	3	2	N E A R S H O R E
	Planet	Cultural	Political	Family	Interpersonal	
	all life	all human life	institutional life	family life	friendship life	

Approaching the island from the far shore, there was fear of encountering dragons, sea monsters, which would diminish noble aims, reducing them to immediate, small-minded concerns. Approaching the island from the near shore, there were fears of encountering dragons, sea monsters, which would inflate everything to large impersonal size.

And yet suppose, as in the best of stories, that monsters turn out to be friends in disguise, that the dragons of the deep need not be killed (as in Western myths) but can be perceived in their beneficent form, the dragons of the East.[12] This can happen because of positioning institutions within the domains.

On one side, the cultural domain stresses criteria for human living. Such a vision can be a strong remedy, counteracting diminution of aim. Beneficent dragons of the far shore can connect the cultural with the institutional domain.

On the other side, the family domain, as we shall see, keeps us in mind of the particularity and uniqueness of persons. Such a vision, stressing the aesthetic order, particularity and time, can be a strong remedy, counteracting the abstractness and impersonality of institutions. Beneficent dragons of the near shore can connect the institutional with the family domain.

Finally, by placing the institutional and political realm between the planetary and the (inter)personal, we insure that *task* will have to be held in the widest, global context. We are reminded of the officials and the functions needed for healthy functioning. We begin to sense that friendship and self-cultivation remain significant in the fourth domain.

The ancients do not draw the sharp *private vs. public* distinction to which we are accustomed. Thus, the relation of *sovereign-to-minister* bears important analogies with the relationships of the family domain. In the next chapter, these relationships will claim our attention.

Notes

1 See the poem "Thoughts on the Way from the Capital to Fengxian," in *Selected Poems of Du Fu*, trans. Li Weijian, revised by Weng Xianliang (Sichuan People's Publishing House, n.d.) The poem appears to have been written late in A.D. 755 , after the Tartar rebellion broke out.

2 See Edmund L. Pincoffs, *Quandries and Virtues: Against Reductivism in Ethics* (Lawrence, KS: University Press of Kansas, 1986). Also see Stanley Hauerwas, *Truthfulness and Tragedy* (Notre Dame: University of Notre Dame Press, 1977) and *A Community of Character* (Notre Dame: University of Notre Dame Press, 1981).

3 See Peter L. Berger and Thomas Luckmann, *The Social Construction of Reality: A Treatise in the Sociology of Knowledge* (Garden City, NY: Doubleday and Company, 1967).

4 I first heard this formulation from William Sloan Coffin, although I believe it derives from Walter Brueggmann. For more, see Walter Brueggmann et al., *To Act Justly, Love Tenderly, Walk Humbly* (Mahwah, NJ: Paulist Press, 1986).

5 Analects, 2:11. My rendering.

⁶ See Hall and Ames, *Thinking Through Confucius*, p. 136; pp.131-38 are relevant.

⁷ Hall and Ames acknowledge this. See *ibid.*, p. 137.

⁸ In Confucius' time, the Chou realm was, as Charles Hucker says, "a European-style group of nation-states in all but name." The king's authority was more titular than real; often a hegemon from one of the eight or so states would keep the loose confederation together. Near Mencius' death, devastating wars increased, and ability came to be ranked above pedigree. See Charles O. Hucker, *China to 1850: A Short History* (Stanford, CA: Stanford University Press, 1978), pp. 37 ff.

⁹ For an alternative approach, see Warren Bennis and Burt Nanus, *Leaders: The Strategies for Taking Charge* (New York: Harper and Row, 1985) and make the following correlations: "attention through vision" — sovereign; "meaning through communication" — first minister; "trust through positioning" — general; and "deployment of self" (innovative learning) — minister of deep waters. Note also the functions as characteristics of individual leaders and as institutionalized in empowering organizations. For a critique of the Bennis and Nanus analysis, see the chapter by Ronald A. Heifetz and Riley M. Sinder, entitled "Political Leadership: Managing the Public's Problem Solving," in Robert Reich, ed. *The Power of Public Ideas* (Cambridge, MA: Ballinger, 1988), pp. 180-203.

¹⁰ See D. C. Lau, trans., *Mencius* (New York: Penguin Books, 1980), IV B:29.

¹¹ *Ibid.*, IV A:9.

¹² Dragons in Western mythology are generally evil; knights such as St. George ride out to kill them. Dragons in the East are benign and beneficent. See Wolfram Eberhard, *A Dictionary of Chinese Symbols* (New York: Routledge and Kegan Paul, 1986).

CHAPTER ELEVEN

THE FAMILY DOMAIN: GENERATIONAL GIFTS AND WOUNDS

Marriage is the most important act in life.
It is the seed of all future existence.

— *Old Chinese saying*

The house in Newport, on the corner of Powell Avenue and Hope Street, belonged to my grandparents, John Peter and Nellie Greenfelder. My grandparents, my father and mother, my sister and I all lived there. It was the household I grew up in, during the 1940s and 1950s. Later, my father and mother bought a farmhouse in the neighboring country-side. We moved, and my grandparents came with us.

For all practical purposes, we were born — my sister and I — in my grandparents' house; my grandparents died in my parents' house. I realize now what I took for granted then — what a gift it was to grow up in a three generational household.

Times are different now. My sister, my mother and I live in three different states. I have married, divorced, and remarried. My daughter lives in two houses in two nearby cities. She has her own gifts and wounds, as do we all. I am more present to her than my father was to me; she, on the other hand, lives a more disparate life than did I.

Throughout history, families have taken many forms, and new forms continue to evolve. During the present epoch, in the United States alone, we see a plurality of childrearing arrangements. Consider, as a sample, two parent and single parent households; natural and adoptive children; step-parents and grandparents raising children; gay, lesbian and collective parenting. Non-kin as well as kin enter our understanding of family. Anthropologist Carol Stack could not find "families" as traditionally defined when she sought them in neighborhoods of urban black poor. To understand this world, she redefined "family" as "the smallest organized, durable network of kin and non-kin who interact daily, providing the domestic needs of children and assuring their survival."[1]

In this chapter, I make no case for one single form of family and am suspicious of any facile ideology of family.[2] In what follows, my intent is first to understand the old on its own terms and then to offer analogues sufficiently open to allow application to many diverse forms of families.

A. Defining the Family Domain

Sometimes, simple ideas can strike one as a major insight. In studying Confucius, I came upon such a simple idea. It is this: *to understand family, one must think of family as ranging over at least three generations — from grandparents to parents to children.* Furthermore, the standpoint for appreciating the three generations is *the middle standpoint* — the standpoint of adults who are also parents, who stand between their parents and their children, between their ancestors and their posterity. No matter whether the individuals live far or near; no matter whether the grandparents or parents or even certain children are alive or dead. To understand family, we must stand in the midst of generations — between those who came before us and those who come after us.

Generational time is a first key to understanding family. Generational line — the transmitting of life — is a second key.

At the heart of the family is *the task of transmitting life* from one generation to the next. Having children is a most concrete way to see this transmission of life. But whether one has biological children or no, the story of family centers on *parents and children.* Generativity — to use Erik Erikson's word — finds its core in this act of giving birth, of creatively transmitting life.[3] There are, of course, many ways to give birth, many ways of creatively transmitting life. At a certain stage of life, we turn toward "the children," come in touch with the mentor/caretaker in us, and think, like the founders of the United States, of ourselves and our posterity.

The community or structural aspect of family I shall specify by *analogues* to the *three* Confucian family relationships.[4] The three familial relationships are best seen in the context of all five of the Confucian relationships along with their accompanying virtues:[5]

Ruler-Minister	———————	yi	—	Righteousness
Parent-Child	———————	ch'in	—	Affection
Husband-Wife	———————	pieh	—	Separate Function
Elder Sibling-Younger Sibling	———	hsü	—	Order
Friend-Friend	———————	hsin	—	Faithfulness

Notice that the ruler-minister relationship finds its home in the institutional domain; the friend-friend relationship, in the interpersonal domain. But the central three relationships belong to the family domain. We shall explore these three: *parent-child*; *husband-wife*; and *elder sibling-younger sibling*.

Our procedure, as already mentioned, is first to understand these relationships in one classical model of family and then to open up the relationships beyond that model.[6]

B. One Classical Notion of Family

When my daughter was very young, she was playing by herself with some brightly colored autumn leaves. I overheard her saying: "This is the mommy leaf. This is the daddy leaf. These are the children."

I note this simply because it is so ordinary. Arranging the world in the image of a family is very old and very young. In China, the Great Declaration of the *Book of History* proclaims: "Heaven and Earth is the parent of all creatures . . . and the great sovereign is the parent of the people."[7]

The *Book of Changes* (*I Ching*) has an intricate way of representing process. The primary polarity of yin-yang is represented by lines:

A yin line is an open line, written thus: — —
A yang line is continuous, written thus: ———

Sets of three such lines are called *trigrams*. There are eight trigrams. These eight trigrams are looked at both as energies of nature and as members of a family. The family has a father and mother, three daughters and three sons. Here are the associations:

The Father (*Ch'ien -* the Heavens)	Eldest Son (Thunder)	Middle Son (Deep Waters)	Youngest Son (the Mountain)
—————— —————— ——————	— — — — ——————	— — —————— — —	—————— — — — —

The Mother (*K'un -* the Earth)	Eldest Daughter (Wind)	Middle Daughter (Fire)	Youngest Daughter (the Lake)
— — — — — —	—————— —————— — —	—————— — — ——————	— — —————— ——————

The primal powers of the heavens and the earth (the creative and receptive) join in order that all the kin, all the ten thousand things, may come to be. Thus, the parent-child relationship is centrally and always about *giving birth and nourishing life*. The family members are also ordered in the elder-younger relationships among the siblings.

Yet even here we do not have a full representation of the family in its intergenerational life. The following illustration widens the picture yet further.

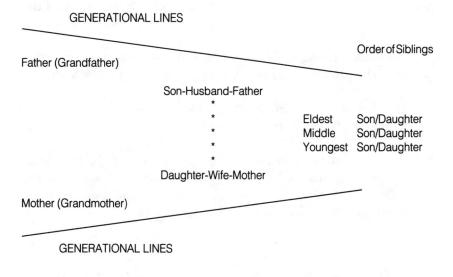

C. Opening up the Three Familial Relationships

Notice that while I have been speaking of parent-child, traditional Confucians spoke of father-son; parent-child has its unisex advantages and avoids the problem of who gets top billing. Nonetheless, there are advantages in employing the language of mother/father and daughter/son. In triadic form, I am child of my parents and parent of my child. I who stand in the middle of generations am child and parent. There is a sense in which I am always my parents' child. However, I am not always a child. I leave childhood behind when I grow up. To think of son and daughter is better. My sister is always her father and mother's daughter; I am always their son. I do not outgrow being son in the way I outgrow being child.

Both my sister and I have children of our own — some biological, some adopted. I am parent and stepparent. One of my stepsons and his wife have chosen not to have children of their own. Nonetheless, they too tend the next generation.

Husband and wife, in the older Confucian scheme, are again seen primarily in generational time and generational line. Husband and wife provide interfamily linking and serve differentiated intrafamilial function.[8] Thus, the *Analects* of Confucius note the special skills needed to relate properly to one's in-laws without alienating one's own family of blood.[9] Seen intergenerationally, the husband and wife link families, have children, and tend ancestors and progeny in terms of differentiated functions. In ancient times, the husband-wife relationship easily blurs into the ideal of father-mother (or, more properly, son & father/daughter & mother); in modern times, wife-husband easily blurs into the ideal of friend-friend.

Lastly, there is order among siblings. If I come from a large enough family, I may be eldest or middle or youngest brother, eldest or middle or youngest sister. If I come from a family of at least two children, I will have and be a brother or sister.

Four terms characterize the three relationships. Thus, I can say: I am son, brother, husband, father. My sister can say: I am daughter, sister, wife, mother.

The family domain is one where one can speak all or some of these names.[10] And we do, whether in biologically based or more extended usage, place ourselves in families. We do find our parents (or caretakers) present in us and we in them. We do consider "the children" and take responsibility for the next generation.

Thus broadened, the three relationships become nodal points in the work of tending generations. In ancient times, the primary focus was filial piety which meant tending one's parents during their life and continuing to honor them after their death.[11] In modern times, the primary focus of parenting looks to the children and their future.[12] The intergenerational work of family has place for tending both ancestors and descendants.

D. THE INTERGENERATIONAL FAMILY AND EDUCATION IN VIRTUE

Suppose we take seriously the sense of standing in the midst of at least three generations. In this context, consider the Golden Rule as Confucius gives it: "Do not impose on others what you yourself do not desire." [13]

In the West, we tend to see the Golden Rule *dyadically* and *abstractly*. The dyad is the unit of two, the pair; the pair is typically given as two (abstract) "anybodies." Western philosophers such as Kant have explored this idea of Golden Rule reciprocity. One learns "reversibility tests" such as "Can I approve this action whether I am on the doer side or on the receiver side?" Such reversibility operates over a dyad, a pair — as if two people stood holding opposite ends of a stick, then reversing.[14] The two people can be any two humans without reference to who they are or in what domain they find themselves.

For the family relations, we must think *triadically* and *concretely*. In simple fashion, the triad consists of

my parents	myself	my children
A	B	C

The Confucian Golden Rule is like an analogy A:B :: B:C.

How I treat my parents is a *model* of how my child learns to treat me. ("C" learns to treat "B" as "B" has come to treat "A".)

I am reminded: do not do to my parent what I would not wish my child to do to me. The model is close at hand.[15] Here we have a Golden Rule for grown-ups who are both child to a parent and parent to a child.

It is *not* a two-place/two-person wheel. The image is *not* that I am now child and later parent and then we exchange places — my parent becoming a child again. My parent always remains my parent; my elder sister or brother always remains my elder. Our practice, where it occurs, of treating the old as if they were little children would be profoundly distasteful to Confucius; it shows a lack of reverence and respect for who they are and a lack of awareness of where we stand.

Consider another triadic relationship:
Sovereign — First Minister — Subminister.

How I (the First Minister) treat my sovereign (as his/her minister) is a *model* of how my ministers learn to treat me.

I am reminded: do not do to my ruler what I would not wish my ministers to do to me. The model is close at hand. Here we have a golden rule for grown-ups who both exercise authority and are subject to authority.

In both cases, there is mutuality over the triad:

[Parent <—> (Child & Parent) <—> Child]
[Ruler <—> (Minister & Ruler) <—> Minister]

In other words, occupying the center, I must model how to treat my children as well as how to honor my parents. As a government minister I stand in the center of a triad and must model how to be with my superiors and how to be with my subjects. (This holds more, not less, strongly of the great sovereign who holds the mandate from heaven and earth. For the Sovereign has human parents and dynastic predecessors and, finally, heaven and earth as parents.) Finally, all stand in service to the people as subjects whose welfare is mirrored by heaven and earth.)[16]

Confucius taught the startling doctrine that nobility was available to all. He also taught that nobility has its obligations (*noblesse oblige*). Triadically speaking, the center position has its duties toward both sides and both sides have duties towards the center. More deeply still, our nobility arises out of our place in the dance, our position in the networks of relations. Furthermore, when concreteness of focus is added to intergenerational time, there is a sense in which we never lose our position, our place in the chain of life. A United States president who leaves office is still a former president and is addressed as such. My father and mother are still my father and mother no matter what. Where time is honored, persons are neither interchangeable nor obsolete. They always remain a part of the institutions they have served and the families of which they remain a part.

From the family, we learn how to relate to our own generation of brothers and sisters, learning to exemplify excellence in oneself and defer to it in others.[17] Lastly, it is in the family that we have our first instruction in being husband or wife. We learn to be husband or wife (for good and ill) from the way our parents were husband and wife; our children learn, in important ways, how to be husband and wife from us. From this intergenerational point of view, divorce and remarriage raise issues of new family alliances and step-parenting. They may also offer a new model of husband-wife relationship.[18]

Three points deserve mention:

First, when we think intergenerationally, the person-in-the-center experiences a Janus-like position and faces two distinct relationships. Education in virtue requires that we acknowledge excellences on both sides and exemplify excellences for both sides.

A second point concerns concreteness and uniqueness. Insofar as there are positions, some general duties or virtues have a place. Insofar as the positions are filled by flesh and blood people in particular domains, there is focus on the concrete over the abstract, on the unique rather than the interchangeable.[19] In the triad of my parents, myself and my children, the persons are not just disembodied "anyones," not just faceless, nameless place-holders. They are real people with faces and temperaments, with a place in space and time. They are my mother, my father, my husband, my wife, my daughter, my son.

Thirdly, the Confucian tradition makes distinctions, but not strong separations between the ethical and the political, between the familial and the institutional. Confucius notes:

> The exemplary person works at the roots, for where
> the roots are firmly set, the Tao will grow forth.
> Filial piety and fraternal deference — these are the
> roots of becoming a person.[20]

The Confucian suspicion of abstract, universal love is well-known. In this tradition, virtue begins at home but does not end there. The concrete lessons learned in the family are extendible beyond the family. The Master said of one of his students that he had the way of the gentleman in four ways: being respectful in his manner of conducting himself, reverent in service of his lord, generous in caring for the common people and just in employing their services.[21] Such virtues have their roots in filial piety and in brotherly and sisterly deference.

Of course, family life is not without its dangers. D. H. Lawrence spoke of an egoism of the couple (*egoisme à deux*). So also can there be an egoism of family or state.[22] The skill is to provide an anchoring of social relation in daily reality and yet encourage step-by-step inclusiveness. The triadic structure, the sense of ongoing relations and Confucius' constant call to service and nobility provide a fruitful place to start.

E. GENERATIONAL GIFTS AND WOUNDS

In the family, the task is the transmission of life. In doing this, we transmit both gifts and wounds.

We, in the United States, have become increasingly conscious of the many forms of addiction and how addictions can be passed from generation to generation. The notion of addiction is widely defined to include substance (or ingestion) addictions and process addictions.[23] Add co-dependence, and we have a net so vast as to catch everyone. We will all turn out to be addicts of differing sorts and degrees.

Addictive patterns prevent us from coming to life more fully. We inherit and pass on such patterns. With them, we also pass on the evasions (denials, projections, repressions, etc.) with which we defend against health.

The wounds of parenting tend to reproduce themselves. When the children become parents, they tend to reproduce the pattern. Wounds of the husband-wife relation tend to reproduce themselves. When the children marry, they tend to reproduce both parent-child and husband-wife patterns. In fact, at times, the husband-wife relation is collapsed into parent-child, or child-child, or parent-parent, as Transactional Analysis reminds us.[24] Husband-wife is but one way to be adult-adult. The relation — as it appears in the family domain — is defined as a division of labor in serving parents and raising children.

Wounds are passed on, yes. And there is a deep sense in which all have been wounded. But gifts are passed on as well and there is an equally profound sense in which all have been gifted. When the gifts become part of us, we call them virtues — powers for living wisely and nobly.

Though it is no easy task, addictions can be defeated. We can say: "Here it stops. We have been an alcoholic family too long. For my sake, for the sake of my parents, the sake of my children, it ceases here."

To think intergenerationally is to bring to mind a wider motivation and a wider sense of self. The Navajo Indians teach that we stand within seven generations. Before we act, they tell us, we must ask: Will this action honor my parents, and grandparents and great grandparents? Will this action benefit my children and grandchildren and great grandchildren? To stand in this place and consciousness is to know one's dignity and the honor that is due to life.

Notes

1. See Carol B. Stack, *All Our Kin* (New York: Harper and Row, 1974), p. 31. Stack's more recent work on return migration from the cities back to North Carolina is explicit in seeing families as intergenerational.

2. In the 1980s, much talk in the United States of "traditional family values" proved to be an ideological cover for renewed assaults against women, the poor and the homeless, gays, blacks and other minorities. Those aware of this are rightly suspicious of canonizing one form of family structure.

3. See Erik H. Erikson, *Childhood and Society* (New York: Norton, 1963) and *Identity: Youth and Crisis* (New York: Norton, 1968).

4. Though the three relations — Parent-Child; Husband-Wife; Elder Sibling-Younger Sibling — are significant clues to establishing the community aspect of this domain; caution is needed in making them constitutive. This is why I speak of analogues to these relationships.

5. See Tu Wei-Ming, *Centrality and Commonality* (Albany, NY: State University of New York Press, 1989), pp. 54-56.

6. In the classical epoch, both West and East, the model of the family tended to be patriarchal. In Western orthodoxies, the father is head of the family; the mother is the heart of the family. In classical China, a somewhat similar image is found. See, for example, the *I Ching* or *Book of Changes*, Wilhelm and Baynes translation (Princeton, NJ: Princeton University Press, 1967), Bollingen Series XIX, Hexagram 37: "The Family," pp. 143-47.

7. Quoted in Alfred Doeblin, *The Living Thoughts of Confucius* (New York: Fawcett World Library, 1959), p. 152.

8. Although I do not discuss what the separate functions of husband and wife might be, I do hold that differentiated function is one thing; its assignment to this or that person, another. Since men and women both possess yin and yang energies, I take it as an open inquiry as to whether the nature of

functions and/or the assignment of functions is gender-linked. It remains an open inquiry whether and how women can "husband" and whether and how men can "wife." For some parallel speculation on the feminine and "mothering," note Sara Ruddick, *Maternal Thinking: Toward a Politics of Peace* (New York: Ballantine books, 1989). For some parallel speculation on the masculine and "fathering," consult the emerging men's movement. See, for example, the Winter and Spring 1990 editions of *Wingspan: Journal of the Male Spirit*, published by the Advantage Group, 11 Beach Street, Suite 4, Manchester, MA 01944.

[9] See, for example, *Analects* I:13.

[10] From these three relationships and four pairs of terms: daughter/son; sister/brother; husband/wife; and father/mother, there also arise other family terms such as aunts, uncles, cousins, in-laws, etc. Given that there are natural and adoptive forms of most of these terms, no one is excluded; everyone is attached to family.

[11] Consider, for example, the *Analects*, chapter one. Consider also *The Book of Filial Duty*, trans. Ivan Chen (London: John Murray, 1920).

[12] See Sara Ruddick, *Maternal Thinking*, for focus on maternal work.

[13] See *Analects* VII:2 and XV:24. Notice that Confucius gives the Golden Rule in a negative ("Do not") formulation. In the first century, A.D., the great Rabbi Hillel would state the rule in a similar way: "What is hateful to you do not do to others — the rest is commentary."

[14] Two points deserve comment. First, such reciprocity has been widely studied by developmentalists such as Piaget (physical reciprocity), Selman (social role-taking) and Kohlberg (moral role-taking). The dyad is the unit used. For Piaget and Kohlberg, see Kegan, *The Evolving Self*, chapter two. Also see Robert L. Selman, *The Growth of Interpersonal Understanding: Developmental and Clinical Analyses* (New York: Academic Press, 1980). Secondly, logic and precedent (equal cases should be treated equally) exert pressure toward universalizability. "Can I approve *any* relevantly similar person doing this action?" For criticism of these moves toward abstractness and substitutability, see Carol Gilligan, *In a Different Voice*.

[15] An old Chinese saying states, "When one is making a hatchet handle with a hatchet, the model is not far off." See *Chung-Yung*, 13. Quoted in Hall and Ames, *Thinking Through Confucius*, p. 286.

[16] See, for example, *Mencius*, V, A:5; see also Hall and Ames, *Thinking Through Confucius*, chapter three.

[17] On deference as a response to recognized excellence, see Hall and Ames, *ibid.*, pp. 181-82.

[18] Though rules and practices differed in the history of China, divorce and remarriage were recognized. Hence, the Husband-Wife relation shares with the Ruler-Minister relation (and the Friend-Friend relation) that there are circumstances when it is proper to break the relation.

[19] The Confucian stress on relationality, concreteness and nonsubstitutability anticipate what are today seen as feminist themes. See Gilligan, *In a Different Voice*. Also Carol Gilligan, Janie Victoria Ward, and Jill McLean Taylor with Betty Bardige, eds., *Mapping the Moral Domain* (Cambridge, MA: Harvard University Press, 1989) and Judith Plaskow and Carol P. Christ, eds., *Weaving the Visions: New Patterns in Feminist Spirituality* (San Francisco: Harper and Row, 1989). On Confucianism as a contextual art (*ars contextualis*), see Hall and Ames, *Thinking Through Confucius*, pp. 131-38 and 246-49.

[20] See *Analects* I:2. The above translation is that of Hall and Ames, *Thinking Through Confucius*, p. 229.

[21] See *Analects* V:16.

[22] Historically, the family system has been lauded for its stability and resilience and criticized for becoming self-centered, nepotistic and an obstacle to good government. For a provocative view on these matters, from an author writing before the Revolution, see Lin Yutang, *My Country and My People* (New York: John Day, 1935), chapters five and six. See also Robert A. Nisbet, *The Quest for Community* (Oxford: England: Oxford University Press, 1953) on the nettlesome question of family in the political thought of the West.

[23] See, for example, Anne Wilson Schaef, *When Society Becomes An Addict* (San Francisco: Harper and Row, 1988), pp. 18-24. In this, Stanton Peele and Archie Brodsky's *Love and Addiction* (New York: Taplinger Publishing, 1975) was a precursor.

[24] See, for example, Eric Berne, *Games People Play* (New York: Grove Press, 1964). Anne Schaef goes so far as to say: "An addictive relationship is, by definition, a *permanent* parent-child/child-parent relationship." See *When Society Becomes an Addict*, p. 28.

CHAPTER TWELVE

THE INTERPERSONAL DOMAIN: THE CIRCLE OF FRIENDS

At dusk I came down from the mountain,
The mountain moon as my companion
. . . .
You took my arm, led me to your hut
. . . .
And I rejoiced at a place to rest
And good wine, too, to pour out with you:
Ballads we sang, the wind in the pines,
Till, our songs done, Milky Way had paled;
And I was drunk and you were merry,
We had gaily forgotten the world!

— *Coming Down from Chung-Nan Mountain*
Li Po *(c. A.D. 701-762)[1]*

Suppose that we too have been coming down a mountain. Having experienced life at the summit — the Tao and the horizon of the planet, we descend through the terrain of human history and pass into the political and family domains. These latter two domains stress task and function. The images are familiar — governing with justice, caring for parents and children with affection, finding differences and commonalities as marriage partners, showing proper respect for brothers and sisters. The duties demanded by official position and family membership are strongly felt in both zones. The terrain is uneven; the paths, steep; the mist rises to make the going careful and cautious. Then suddenly, we break through to another level, below the cloud-like mist. The going becomes easier. We find a friend waiting, a friend who takes our arm and offers "a place to rest and good wine too." Friend with friend, we forget the world!

The relation of friend-friend, marked by trustworthiness, defines a different domain. *The temporal aspect of this domain is the lifetime; the community or structural aspect is a particular dyad — the pair: friend-friend.* In the family domain, we stood in the midst of generations; in the friendship domain, we each stand in the midst of our lives. For my purposes, I will speak about friends who are adults, or who, on the road to adulthood, are conscious of standing within the past, present and future of a lifetime.

Friendship is not task-defined — not, at any rate, in the ways that both the institutional and familial domains are task-defined. Indeed, friendship between adults can be seen as a liberative release (however temporary) from the all-too-pressing obligations of institutional and family tasks.

A. FRIENDSHIP AND THE TIME OF THE LIFETIME

The time of the lifetime dawns gradually. As a young child I live my life as a series of moments. Events come and go like children on a sliding board, like bubbles in the breeze. As a child, I tell my story in similar fashion. This happened and this happened and this happened. A series of sentences joined by "and" — like Lego blocks. I know of today and tomorrow, but "last month" or "next week" or "in a year" or "several years ago" hold only minimal meaning. Grandma and the dinosaurs were surely contemporaries — a long, long time ago.

As I come to age ten and above, I find adults asking troublesome questions such as "What are you going to do with your life?" and "What do you want to be when you grow up?" I realize more clearly that I have a lifetime. I have a past that might have been different. I have a future that is open and unknown. Even my present seems hidden from me, endlessly shifting as I compare myself to others. I often feel embarrassingly out of my control. Who am I? Why do I feel this way? Am I the only one to feel and think and desire as I do? Will I find someone to be my friend? To love me? Will I find a path in the world, someone to be, something valuable to do? What will become of me?

As the time of the lifetime dawns, friendship becomes possible in qualitatively different ways than anything experienced earlier. The psychiatrist Harry Stack Sullivan draws a developmental map, distinguishing the juvenile era of grade school, the preadolescence of middle school, the early adolescence of high school. In Sullivan's scheme, the *juvenile* era is a time to acquire habits of competition, cooperation and compromise. *Preadolescence* — a time of same-sex chumship — opens the need for intimacy — where the two people validate each other's worth. Such intimacy and validation of worth occur in a relationship Sullivan calls "collaboration." Cooperation still centers on "me and my prestige"; collaboration shifts the center to "we."[2] Sullivan places the roots of friendship in preadolescence, the time of "best friends" who share intimate exchange.

When the time of the lifetime opens up and the need for intimacy is newly felt, another person becomes important for his or her own sake. And the relationship takes on a life and value of its own. A mutuality of sharing occurs. We see ourselves through each other's eyes. We share intimate secrets and experience a new sort of feedback. Here is a period when parents are no longer the primary validators, when a new sense of the lifetime is emerging, and when true collaboration becomes possible.

We pause at this moment when intimacy arises, knowing that sexuality will soon enter.[3] Thereafter, the picture is more complex, but friendship and intimacy are no less important. Seeing ourselves through the honest, caring eyes of a friend restores perspective, reinforces esteem, and roots us more fully in the real. Our capacities for love and hurt deepen, and so does our capacity to share our lives as friends.

B. FRIENDSHIP AND THE CONFUCIAN CLASSICS

In the very opening of the Analects (I:1), Confucius exclaims:

> Is it not a pleasure, having learned something, to try it out at due intervals? Is it not a joy to have friends come from afar? Is it not gentlemanly not to take offense when others fail to appreciate your abilities?

In this beautiful beginning, the joy of friendship appears between the pleasure of learning and a gentle nobility that can rise above the pain of not being appreciated. These three — the pleasure, the joy and the gentleness — find support in being shared. Was it not said of old that joy shared is doubled, sorrow shared is halved?

Friendship *(yu)* is the very setting of the *Analects*. Confucius and his students form a circle of friends. In entering the *Analects*, we enter *an ongoing conversation among those already friends*. There is genuine mutuality here. Confucius refuses to consider himself sage and freely acknowledges his own shortcomings.[4] Avoiding speculation about the supernatural or the afterlife, he directs attention to the shared human way, and he delights in the companionship of his students.[5]

Confucius' teaching is decidedly contextual. He responds to a question from this particular student at this particular stage of learning. The answer he gives to one may not be the answer appropriate to another. He learns from students and he teaches them. He uses self-disclosure, songs and sayings of ancient times, particular examples of higher and lesser excellences from the lives of particular people past and present. His feedback, like a medical prescription, is meant for the one needing it. And yet much is learned in overhearing.

For such interchanges, trust is of the essence. Without the conditions of trust and trustworthiness, important personal disclosure and constructive feedback will not flourish.[6] Thus, the virtue associated with friendship is *hsin*, a term that has been translated as loyalty, trust, trustworthiness in what one says, or, as Hall and Ames translate: "living up to one's word."[7] This notion covers a continuum.

At one end of the continuum, trustworthiness links with *doing*, with simplicity in speech and effectiveness in deed. One speaks sparingly and makes what one says count — saying clearly what you will do; carrying out what you say.

At the other end of the continuum, trustworthiness links with *being*, with honesty, sincerity, authenticity.[8] What one says derives from who one is and is becoming; one speaks from the heart without doubleness; one speaks from a readiness to learn, to change, to make one's truth real.

The speaking in Confucius is like the speaking respected by the American Indians. It is less to report than to witness, certify, accredit; less to witness than to bring into being. Here is a speaking that matters. It is performative.[9] And, as with the American Indians, such speaking demands certain conditions for listening — a listening that acknowledges the other, a listening that empties the self of barriers that prevent the other from being heard. Paradoxically, such speaking and listening is a both a condition for and a fruit of friendship.

C. FRIENDSHIP AND THE SEARCH FOR COMMUNITY

In this chapter, we have moved from the modern West to the ancient East. Taking cues from a modern psychiatrist, I gave a view of friendship that stressed intimacy, collaboration and the time of the lifetime. Next, I noted that, in the Confucian tradition, friendship's virtue — *hsin* — is a trust and trustworthiness in speaking and, I would add, in listening. Thus far, new and old complement each other.

In this present section, I will draw a contrast between classical and modern ways of thinking. The difference, as Sir Henry Maine once noted, is *between status and contract*; the difference, I would say, is between taking *connection or separation* as basic.

In the modern view, we begin with *separation as primary*. We think of two self-contained, self-sufficient persons, what Alan Watts would call two "skin-encapsulated egos." We imagine that they are by nature *unrelated*. We invoke *individual self-interest* to get them together. If the individuals choose to unite, it is by acts of the *will* that they do so. The parties consent to *cooperation* (not collaboration); *contract* enforces the arrangement should willingness flag. Such is one possible picture.

In the Chinese classical view, the picture is very different. Humans are, in this worldview, "irreducibly relational" — as, in fact, is every-thing.[10] The primary feature of reality — as we see so clearly in the birthing and tending of children by parents — is affectionate presence. "According to Confucian teaching," writes Thomas Berry, "a mutual attraction of things for each other functions at all levels of reality as the interior binding force of the cosmic, social and personal life."[11] This mutual attraction between all beings can be seen as what we call gravity on the physical plane and love on the human plane.[12]

Suppose we look at friendship in this way. The implications shift radically.

First, on the ancient Chinese account, a person is best thought of not as a "skin-encapsulated ego," but as a focus in a field of relations.[13] Two persons meet as already situated selves, as already rooted in a bioregion, cultural matrix, institutional roles, and family position. These relations, though partly fluid (through creative reinterpretation), are nonetheless relatively *given*. There are cosmological and biological directionalities in place.[14] We enter life at a particular point in the cultural and historical stream, at a particular position in the institutional and familial networks. Structures and their histories predate us. We are born into a world not of our making, where we were not "present at the creation."[15] The bonds are present in outline before we know them; relationships are underway before we choose them. Consent ratifies as much as creates.

Second, if we are each a focus in a field, then both diversity and commonality may be affirmed. Each of us is a different viewpoint on a common or overlapping field. Different viewpoints arise from different backgrounds, different positionality in the domains and different experiences flowing from interactions. Yet the domains are patterns within patterns. Hence, there are common or overlapping fields. Collaboration, not simply cooperation, is possible. For the ancient Chinese, harmony no more means uniformity than a good soup means bland water without diversity of spices.[16]

Third, prior connectedness, not subsequent contract, provides the grounding. Only when that grounding is obscured and common culture ceases to motivate, does force and the threat of force move to the fore.[17]

Friendship, as presented here, ranges over a continuum. With no pretense to completeness, we might distinguish three aspects: *breadth* (the range of interests shared), *length* (the duration of the sharing), and *depth* (how much of the total personalities of each are shared). Consider, as our central example of friendship, an intimate exchange about many matters over considerable time in a collaborative union of some depth. Let the central model exemplify a fairly total sharing. Let the periphery include moments and degrees of "friendship" — even with enemies and strangers (if basic humanity is touched).[18] Between the center and the circumference of friendship's circle, think of the different forms of intimacy possible with acquaintances and neighbors, companions and confidants, co-workers and fellow citizens, lovers and spouses, mothers and fathers, sisters and brothers, sons and daughters, religious and cultural masters, works of human hands and natural places, stars and planets, and the Tao itself. Our friendship and affection, though undoubtedly fostered step by step, can reach as far as our connectedness.

D. Friendship, Freedom and Lao Tzu

Of the friendship domain, Thomas Berry writes:

> [The] friendship community is . . . most important in fostering some of the deepest of all human experiences precisely because it is neither ritualized, nor politicized, nor intellectualized, nor subject to family obligation. It belongs to the order

---

of the greatest freedom and creates a unique intimacy of its own. It is simply that attachment that individual persons and small groups of persons have for each other and the joy they have in their sharing of life and thought and feeling.[19]

I have been accentuating the Confucian insight into the relational nature of reality. In friendship, we see this attachment in a simple and unimpeded way. But while friendship affirms some bonds, it also liberates us from others. In this release from duty, in this celebration of freedom, we feel once again the presence of Lao Tzu.

Lao Tzu's way is more radical than Confucius' way. Confucius extends common sense and moves to solutions. Lao Tzu overturns common sense and praises dissolutions. Like the Sermon on the Mount, Lao Tzu's path of radical simplicity seems hardly welcome "in" the world.

Lao Tzu stresses letting go, noninterference, *wei wu wei* — acting by not-acting. This is not a counsel of complete inaction, rather it is a call to a depth beneath the usual dualisms, and a patience to await the opportune moment.

Friendship does indeed require trustworthiness — trust in ourselves, in our friends and in the mutual conversation that we are. Lao Tzu asks us to go deeper — beyond the labels, beyond what we think we know — into not-knowing, into a place beyond words. Here is a trust beyond trust — an experienced assurance that already we are at one; already the great pattern is moving between and through us. Nonjudgment and noninterference are rooted in such trust.

In the Tibetan tradition, this trust is likened to the "Great Eastern Sun" within us. It is named Great because it is primordial, without conditions, always present — even on cloudy days and stormy seasons. It is called Eastern because the sun rises in the East, and the Great Eastern Sun is a rising sun, a trust in the possibility of continual renewal. Finally, this trust is likened to the sun because it gives light and warmth and life.[20] Awareness of and trust in this fundamental worth is most relevant to friendship.

E. FRIENDSHIP AND THE REALM OF THE ARTISTS

Thomas Berry speaks wisely in saying that "the friendship community comes to its fullest expression in the poets."[21] Henry Wei writes: "While Confucianism manifests its influence mainly in the ethical and the political sphere, Taoism manifests its influence in the literary, the artistic, and the spiritual."[22] Chinese poetry, painting and calligraphy have imbibed deeply the spirit of the Tao. In this brief section, I shall only suggest the richness here.[23]

A Chinese verse from the eighth century sets the meditative mood:

> The wild geese fly across the long sky above
> Their image is reflected upon the chilly water below.
> The geese do not mean to cast their image on the water;
> Nor does the water mean to hold the image of the geese.[24]

Li P'o strikes a similar note of natural harmony:

> You ask me why should I stay in this blue mountain,
> I smile but do not answer. O, my mind is at ease!
> Peach blossoms and flowing streams pass away without
>   trace.
> How different from the mundane world![25]

A certain sort of sharing emerges from the cultivation of such sensitivity. Here is a sample in a poem by Wang Wei:

> Lately I became aware of the meaning of Quietude.
> Day after day I stayed away from the multitude.
> I cleaned my cottage and prepared it for the visit of a monk
> Who came to me from the distant mountains.
> He descended from the cloud-hidden peaks
> To see me in my thatched house.
> Sitting in the grass we shared the resin of the pine.
> Burning incense we read the sutra of Tao.
> When the day was over we lighted our lamp.
> The temple bells announced the beginning of the evening.
> Suddenly I realized that Quietude is indeed Joy,
> And I felt that my life has abundant leisure.[26]

Friendship, as Thomas Berry reminded us, is given fullest expression by the poets. I opened this chapter with the poet Li P'o (A.D. 701-762) coming down from Mount Chung-Nan and visiting a friend. I close this chapter with another poet, Li Po contemporary, Wang Wei (A.D.

701-761), who writes of the same mountains and the friendly feeling they inspire.

> Since the days of my middle life
> I was deeply devoted to Tao.
> Recently I came to live
> In the mountains of Chung-nan.
> Oftentimes — with joy in my heart —
> Alone, I roam here and there.
> It is a wonderful thing
> That I am aware of myself.
> When the streamlet ends my trip
> I settle down and catch
> The moment of rising mists.
> Now and then I meet
> A furrowed dweller of the woods.
> We chat and laugh;
> Never do we want to go home.[27]

From here, where we are also friend to ourself, we easily move within — into the space where self-cultivation resides.

Notes

[1] The full title is "Coming Down from Chung-Nan Mountain by Hu-Szu's Hermitage, He Gave Me Rest for the Night and Set Out Wine," quoted from Arthur Cooper, trans., *Li Po and Tu Fu* (New York: Penguin Books, 1973), p. 151.

[2] See Harry Stack Sullivan, *Conceptions of Modern Psychiatry* (New York: W.W. Norton, 1966), p. 55. Also see Sullivan, *Interpersonal Theory of Psychiatry*, edited by Helen Swick Perry and Mary Ladd Cawel (New York: W.W. Norton, 1953), pp. 246 ff. In the developmental map of Lawrence Kohlberg, the move from cooperation/competition to collaboration occurs in the move from stage two to stage three. See Lawrence Kohlberg, *Essays on Moral Development. Vol. I: The Philosophy of Moral Development: Moral Stage and the Idea of Justice* (San Francisco: Harper and Row, 1981) and also Kegan, *The Evolving Self.*

3 From early adolescence on, Sullivan sees three needs combining and colliding: (i) "the need for personal security — that is, for freedom from anxiety [or positively, maintenance of self-esteem and personal worth]; (ii) the need for intimacy — that is, for collaboration with at least one other person [connected also with the avoidance of loneliness]; and (iii) the need for lustful satisfaction, which is connected with genital activity in pursuit of the orgasm." See Sullivan, *Interpersonal Theory of Psychiatry*, p. 264.

4 See *Analects* VII:34 on the first point; *Analects* V:9; VII:3; VII:22; IX:8 on acknowledging shortcomings.

5 See *Analects*, XI:12 and XV:29. Also XI:26.

6 On the importance of the conditions of trust, see Jacob Needleman, *The Heart of Philosophy* (New York: Bantam, 1984), chapter three, and Parker Palmer, *To Know as We are Known: A Spirituality of Education* (San Francisco: Harper and Row, 1983). On disclosure and feedback, see the model first presented in 1955 by Joe Luft and Harry Ingham and named the Johari Window. The model is discussed in Joseph Luft, *Group Processes: An Introduction to Group Dynamics* (Palo Alto, CA: National Press Book, 1970), chapter three. See also E.F.Schumacher, 1977, chapters six through nine, on the four fields of knowledge.

7 The term is used forty times in the *Analects*. See Hall and Ames, *Thinking Through Confucius*, p. 60.

8 This sense of trustworthiness is continuous with the notion of *ch'eng* in the *Doctrine of the Mean*. See Tu Wei-Ming, *Centrality and Commonality*.

9 On performatives, see Fingarette, *Confucius*, pp. 11 ff., and Hall and Ames, *Thinking Through Confucius*, pp. 264 ff.

10 The phrase is that of Hall and Ames. See *ibid.*, p. 287. They use the phrase of the achieved person; I use it more widely.

11 Berry, "Affectivity," p.1.

12 See Brian Swimme, *The Universe is a Green Dragon*.

13 For the very useful notion of focus and field, see Hall and Ames, *Thinking Through Confucius*, pp.237-41.

14 See Gibson Winter, *Liberating Creation*.

15 I have nothing theological in mind here. See Berger and Luckmann, *The Social Construction of Reality*, for a plausible view.

16 See Hall and Ames, *Thinking Through Confucius*, pp. 165-66, where they quote Yang Po-chun's reference to the *Tso-chuan*.

17 For Confucius' relation to law and force, see Hall and Ames, *ibid.*, pp. 156 ff.

---

18 In chapter six, I mention the wonderful story of the young aikido student, the drunk and the little old Japanese man. See Ram Dass and Gorman, *How Can I Help?*, pp. 167-71.

19 Berry, "Affectivity," p. 10.

20 See Chogyam Trungpa, *Shambhala*, especially chapters six and seven.

21 Berry, "Affectivity," p. 10.

22 *Ibid.*, p. 10.

23 See, for example, Chang Chung-Yuan, *Creativity and Taoism: A Study of Chinese Philosophy, Art and Poetry* (New York: Harper and Row, 1963) and Frederick Franck, *Art as a Way* (New York: Crossroad Publishing, 1981).

24 This poem from the Zenrin Kushu is quoted in Chang Chung-Yuan, *Creativity*, p. 57.

25 Quoted *ibid.*, p. 90.

26 Quoted *ibid.*, p. 185.

27 Quoted *ibid.*, pp. 177-78.

CHAPTER THIRTEEN

THE PERSONAL DOMAIN: ATTENDING TO THE MOVEMENTS OF THE HEART

*From the Son of Heaven down to the mass of the people,
all must consider the cultivation of the person
the root of everything besides.*
— *The Great Learning*[1]

In all of us, there is a center of connectedness, an original mind, a true nature, a compassionate heart. This core of life can be forgotten and remembered and forgotten, found and lost and found. Mencius has said:

> When people lose a dog or chicken, they realize that they should get it back. But when they lose their mind or heart, they do not realize that they should recover it.[2]

Cultivation of two sorts is required:

(a) the giving and receiving that finds its field of practice in the Confucian five relations, and

(b) the letting go and letting be that finds its model in the Taoist path.

Confucius' way is the way of form, of careful (and care-filled) distinctions, the way of naming and renaming, to serve wisely and nobly the family-based world.

Lao Tzu's way is the pathless path of emptiness, of letting go of distinctions, of returning to the mind of the child, to the infinite, to the uncarved block.[3]

But the yin and yang of Lao Tzu and Confucius must not be taken in too static a fashion. Confucius, while training leaders, is committed to inner work; Lao Tzu, while stressing inner work, speaks to leaders about governing.[4] Both could affirm the aim of this book: "to come to life more fully so as to serve life more wisely and more nobly — sageliness within, kingliness without."

The "space" of the personal domain is the space of inner work, of self-cultivation, the work of realizing — making real, becoming real, rejoicing in the real.[5] The space of inner work is the total body-mind/heart-spirit that we are. The self, while rooted in our unique body, is expandable — able to identify with larger communions, able to embody the domain where the inner work is focused. *The time of the personal domain is the time of the moment, the present — presentness, presence, being present.* Only by being present can inner work be done, and being present is itself a part of the work.

A. The Personal Domain in Relation to the Other Domains

The domains are seven. We might think of the first and seventh domain as the "embracing domains." On this account, the remaining five domains are "embraced" by self and Tao. When we think of our self as our embodied self, we realize that the cycles of energy move in us — in our very body — as well as around us. When we think of the self as mystery, we think of self as mirroring the Tao and all that the Tao encompasses.

1. The First and Seventh Domains

The first and seventh domains have certain likenesses. There is a mysterious unnameable quality about both the self and the Great Ultimate (Tao or *Theos*). When the self is whole, it is transparent, like no-self, a spacious welcoming presence. Similar to the self becoming no-self, the Tao is transparent, disappearing into a world that is vividly and sacredly itself. It is then the deep down inwardness of all things[6] and the spacious welcoming void where all things arise unhindered and return unjudged.

To talk "about" Tao or God is like talking "about" the self. It is like trying to capture the ocean with a child's pail, like the eye trying to see itself (rather than "sourcing" the seeing), like "trying to stop an echo by shouting at it," as the Zen masters say. In Martin Buber's terms, talking "about" God is acting as if the Eternal Thou were just another "it."[7] So, talking about myself is talking about a fiction, a figure of the past, treating the Active "I" as if it were simply a "me," another "it."

Meister Eckhart said: "The eye with which I see God is the same eye as the eye with which God sees me."[8] In truth, there is only the seeing, the awareness, the emptiness in which all things arise, flourish and return to their source. The first and seventh domains do not so much reflect each other; rather they become a transparent context where all the other domains have the space to be and to be appreciated.

2. The Personal Domain and the Five Intermediate Domains

There is a tradition in the West and the East wherein the inner space of the person is described as having a complexity (a set of parts) which can be in conflict or in harmony.[9] At the roots of this view is the teaching that the human is a microcosm reflecting the larger macrocosm. As above, so below. As without, so within. I suggest that the self as complex can be seen on the model of each of the five intermediate domains: friendship, family, kingdom, human culture, and the earth with all its beings. Consider each domain in turn.

In the interpersonal domain, we are in or out of one-to-one relations with individuals. So, within the self as complex, we can be enemy or friend to ourself.[10] As without, so within.

In the three-generational family domain, we stand between our parents and our children. Transactional Analysis sees each person as having a parent-adult-child within.[11] Carl Jung notes that each person has a Husband and Wife within.[12] No doubt, we also carry our siblings within. As without, so within.

In the institutional domain, the twelve officials appear. As their good or ill-functioning shows up in the kingdom without, so also it is manifest in the kingdom of the body-mind-spirit.[13] As without, so within.

In the cultural domain, we are the myths and rituals of our tribe, the cultural scripts of our people. In fact, all of the epochs reside within us. And, in knowing the light and the darkness of each epoch, we can say with the Roman playwright Terrence: "I am human and nothing human is alien to me."[14]

In the earth domain, we move beyond the human-centered. As the shamans have known, we bear within us the animals, the trees, the elements. In the words of Chief Seattle: "All things are connected like the blood that unites us all. Man did not weave the web of life, he is merely a strand in it. Whatever he does to the web, he does to himself."[15]

In truth, the self is both complex and not complex. As complex, it mirrors the intermediate five domains and can find disharmony or harmony in any and all. As not-complex, the self is as the Tao is. Tasting both the timeless self and the self in time gives self-cultivation its two-fold aspect.

B. SELF-CULTIVATION: THE ETHICAL AND THE SPIRITUAL

It is often said that Confucius is an ethical teacher par excellence, while Lao Tzu and the Taoists move toward the way of ego-dissolution, the way of less and less until the Tao is all. But, neither man shared the framework of modern ethics, with its strong separations between (i) *Is* vs. *Ought*, (ii) *Self* vs. *Others*, and (iii) *Private* vs. *Public*.

First, neither sage speaks the language of *is* vs. *ought*. Both Confucius and Lao Tzu are, in different ways, "ought-aversive."

Confucius does not speak the language of *is* vs. *ought*. He speaks about the superior (exemplary or profound) person and the small-minded (perhaps, still growing) person. Both are possibilities within us, because nobility is open to all.[16] In Confucius' view, we are already on the path, on a way most human: caring for our children, honoring our parents, supporting our friends. Sometimes, we do these things more consciously and consistently, more effectively and joyously than at other times, but we are already and always involved in life. Furthermore, Confucius emphasizes exemplars of excellence over principles, relationships and rituals over rules, and encourages learning, flexibility, and appropriateness throughout.[17]

Lao Tzu stands even farther from the language of *is* vs. *ought*. His stinging critique of morality is well-known.[18] He notes how counter-productive any moral (or legal) codes are. What is required is a return to the Tao, to nature's way (which Alan Watts calls the Watercourse Way). To return to one's original nature can be done because one's original nature is always present. To come to this nature requires radical simplification, letting go of desires, practicing noninterference.

Second, neither sage saw a radical separation between *self* and *others*, between the *selfish* and the *altruistic*. Confucius teaches that one establishes oneself by establishing others and, in establishing others, one establishes oneself.[19] Furthermore, Lao Tzu could have approved the saying of the twelfth-century Japanese Zen Master Dogen:

> To study the Way is to study the Self.
> To study the Self is to forget the Self.
> To forget the Self is to be enlightened by all things.
> To be enlightened by all things is to remove the barrier
>   between Self and Other.[20]

Third, neither sage made a radical separation between the *private* and the *public*, between the *personal* and *political*. For Confucius, training the noble person *is* training a person for leadership. And Lao Tzu speaks often about wise ruling, commending noninterference (*wu wei*) to ruler and subject alike.

Both masters shared the ancient saying: sageliness within; kingliness without — *nei sheng; wai wang*. Looking at the sweep of Chinese history, we are correct to note certain tendencies: the city and court are associated with the Confucians; the mountain retreats, with the Taoists. Also we are correct to see dispositions toward imbalances: to see rule-following, rigidity, empty ceremony, as a Confucian tendency to imbalance; to see the search for magic remedies and a dreamlike withdrawal as a Taoist tendency to imbalance. But a simple "ethics vs. spiritual" distinction will not do. Self-cultivation in both traditions moves from surface to depth; self-cultivation in both traditions tends toward the action arising out of and returning to meditative stillness.[21] The differences between East and West, outlined in chapter one, remain true when we consider Confucius and Lao Tzu.

In summary, I offer the following reminders:

1) Self-cultivation is not cultivation of some modern isolated, unconnected, self-sufficient self. Self-cultivation is of the expansive self that is also the domains.

2) Self-cultivation does not occur in a context that separates self and others. Establishing self and others arise together.

3) Self-cultivation does not occur in a context where the private is separated from the public and the personal separated from the political. The domains are continuous, one with the other.

4) Self-cultivation does not proceed in linear fashion, as if one had to become whole before aiding family or world. Rather movement in

any domain opens possibility in all others.

    5)   Self-cultivation is addressed to the superior person in us, calling us to practice human-heartedness, calling us to let go of barriers.

C. SELF-CULTIVATION AND THE GREAT LEARNING

    One of the Confucian classics, *The Great Learning* (*Ta Hsueh*), will provide a summary of what we have said and will point the way forward. *The Great Learning* is addressed to the Sovereign (or the superior or exemplary or profound person in us). The aim of the work is (a) to make manifest illustrious virtue, (b) to renew the people, and thus (c) to abide in the highest excellence. The aim may be understood in two ways (a more Confucian call to virtues or a more Taoist return to our deep nature):[22]

To practice virtues	To show forth one's heaven-bestowed nature
and, in so doing, to love the people	and, in so doing, renew the people's nature
causing all to rest in the highest excellence.	causing all to rest in the highest excellence.

    In both modes of understanding, the structure remains the same — *chung-shu*. In other words, conscientiousness in working on self (*chung*) is linked with mutuality (*shu*), involving others. Such inner-outer, self-other work is done so that the whole may abide in the highest good.

The core of this brief classic is as follows:

> The ancients who wished to show forth illustrious virtue throughout the Empire (or world), first ordered well their own states.
> Wishing to order well their states, they first regulated their families.
> Wishing to regulate their families, they first cultivated their persons.
> Wishing to cultivate their persons, they first rectified their hearts.
> Wishing to rectify their hearts, they first sought to be sincere in their thoughts.
> Wishing to be sincere in their thoughts, they first extended to the utmost their knowledge.

Such extension of knowledge lay in the investigation of things.
Things being investigated, knowledge became complete.
Their knowledge being complete, their thoughts were sincere.
Their thoughts being sincere, their hearts were then rectified.
Their hearts being rectified, their persons were cultivated.
Their persons being cultivated, their families were regulated.
Their families being regulated, their states were rightly governed.
Their states being rightly governed, the whole Empire (or world)
   was made tranquil and happy.

From the Son of Heaven down to the mass of the people,
   all must consider the cultivation of the person
   the root of everything besides.[23]

The structure of this sequence, sometimes given as the "eight points," can be simplified to seven by combining "the extension of knowledge" with "the investigation of things." The "3-1-3" picture thus obtained can be likened to a tree with roots below and branches above:

Empire or world   correlates with our domains 6 & 5 — the planetary (all
                           earth life) and the cultural (all human life) domains[24]

State   correlates with our domain 4 — the institutional
                           or kingdom domain

Family   correlates with our domains 3 & 2
                           (the family domain to which we
                           here link the friendship domain)

. . . .

PERSONAL CULTIVATION

. . . .

Rectification of the Heart

Sincerity of Thoughts

Extension of Knowledge through Investigation of Things

Let us begin with the three roots of the tree.

First there is an *inquiry* — an inquiry into life, an inquiry that will make a difference to our thinking and acting.[25] Inquiry is a self-correcting process of experiencing, understanding, affirming, valuing, acting. Inquiry moves beyond fantasy and conjecture to prize the real — *what is* and *what is becoming*. Inquiry is guided by a deep respect for the nature of things, for objectivity, for feedback from the real. Such an inquiry, I would say, is close to the type of inquiry used in traditional Chinese medicine — to see, to hear, to feel, to ask. It is close to the inquiry of the skillful therapist and the skillful diplomat. What is going on? How is life manifesting itself here? How do things originate and grow? What promotes health and what promotes sickness? How are the seeds of future events already showing themselves subtly in present acts and omissions? How am I showing up in all of this? Am I part of the problem or part of the solution? When I act appropriately so as to allow the space for healing, I do not impose the past on the present or force fixity on what is flowing. I listen and learn, act and observe, in an ongoing dialogue with life.

Second, there is *sincerity* (authenticity, honesty with myself). Among the things I come to be aware of is my own participation in my life. As the saying goes: when things go right or wrong for me, there is always one person present — me. If my aim is "to come to life more fully so as to serve life more wisely and more nobly," I must have the courage to see myself, the courage to come to terms with self-deception. My heart is such as to move by nature toward the healthy and the beautiful. I need to hear and acknowledge honestly the prompting of my deeper nature, rather than to drown out these impulses. I need to overcome dualisms and reclaim my original nature. The scholar James Legge observes that, as we grow up, our virtuous nature is perverted "through defects of the physical constitution, through inward lusts, and through outward seductions; and the great business of life should be, to bring the nature back to its original purity."[26] As we recognize, with humor and forgiveness, our own imbalances, we become more whole, more single-minded, less scattered. Knowing, with joy, who we are and what is important, we are no longer double; the outer and the inward person are at one.[27]

Third, there is *rectification of the heart*. Beyond the self-enclosure (which is remedied by investigating things) and the self-deception (which is remedied by self-honesty), there lies our partiality. The word is a good one, indicating that we can be partial through bias and we can be partial through not seeing widely enough. We become partial as the mind is pulled from presentness and balance through the passions. The passions mentioned are anger, fear, fond regard, and sorrow. These emotions are not bad, but they can pull us off balance and introduce a partialness that obscures what needs to be done. Rectifying the heart requires that we go beyond the partiality of either-or. Both "this" and "that" are present — both balance and imbalance, sickness and health, danger and opportunity. Thus, the other side of retaining equilibrium is presentness. *The Great Learning* teaches: "When the mind is not present, we look and do not see; we hear and do not understand; we eat and do not know the taste of what we eat."[28]

At the roots, self-cultivation takes place by inquiry, sincerity, rectification of the heart; in its branches, self-cultivation takes place by rectifying family, state and empire. Perhaps the 3-1-3 picture is misleading. Perhaps I might better have written 3-0-3, for the center is more a mirror that a separate "thing." A tree is not something other than the processes we call roots and branches. So also, self-cultivation is not other than tending roots and tending branches. After tending the roots, we turn to the three branches.

First there is the *family*. The partiality of the uncentered heart will naturally spill over into the realm of family (and friends). Affection, dislike, awe, arrogance, sorrow — all can blind us. Thus, it is said: "there are few [persons] in the world, who love and at the same time know the bad qualities of the object of their love, or who hate and yet know the excellences of the object of their hatred."[29]

Second, there is the *state*. The virtues required earlier for the family also are needed for the state. In the three-generational family, vital needs are met through the virtues of humanity, appropriateness, respect for the depth of rituals, and wise, ongoing learning.[30] These virtues, seen in their depth, are required if we are to be of nourishing, virtue-enhancing service to the sovereign, to the officials, to the people. What is at issue here is what I would call the conditions of C.A.R.E. — Collaborative And Respectful Existence. But these conditions are not different in kind from what is sought in the family, although the virtues must also take root in policies and procedures, rules and rituals, and in those holding the functions of the officials. Conditions of C.A.R.E. are needed both for the family and for the state to "show forth illustrious virtue, so that all can abide in the highest good." Our difficulties with paternalism/maternalism ought not prevent us from appreciating what is needed for "growing people."

Third, there is the *empire* (or the *world*). Today, we speak more easily of the *human community* (including all who have gone before us) and the *earth community* which includes as our kin other species as well as other humans. Even with these vast domains before us, we may address the sovereign (the sovereign in us, the profound person we are and are becoming). As sovereigns of the compassionate heart, we possess a measuring-square to regulate conduct: the rule of reciprocity: what is injurious to us (in our body-mind-spirit), we are not to do to the wider networks of life. Of old, it was promised that right behavior of the sovereign toward the aged and the elders would inspire the people to be filial and deferential, that right behavior toward the young and the helpless would make compassion flourish. Today, when the earth itself is a wounded healer, the virtues need to be extended most fully — to all living beings as our kin, especially to "the least of the brethren," be they humans like ourselves or other species who are our elders in the cosmic story.

The sage-kings saw the people as wounded. When anyone was hungry, that hunger was felt. When anyone drowned, the loss was felt.[31] The heavens identified with the people and reminded the ruler to do so as well, lest the mandate of heaven pass to another. Today, we see the earth itself identified with all its creatures and all its fragile systems. We ourselves must identify as widely as the earth, lest the mandate of the earth remove the conditions of life from us and our children.

Such is the context and range of self-cultivation. Establishing the domains in harmony is establishing ourselves, we who are communal to the core. Is it not indeed true to say then what was said at the start?

> From the Son of Heaven down to the mass of the people,
> all must consider the cultivation of the person
> the root of everything besides.

Notes

[1] The Great Learning, no. 6, from James Legge, *Confucius: Confucian Analects, The Great Learning, and The Doctrine of the Mean* (New York: Dover Press, 1971 — 1st pub. 1893), p. 359.

2 D. C. Lau, trans., *Mencius*, 6 A:11.

3 See the *Tao Te Ching*, chapter 28.

4 See Henry Wei, *The Guiding Light*, for a strong presentation of the views that the *Tao Te Ching* is directed to leaders and that Lao Tzu is explicitly teaching a meditative path.

5 For a similar view, see the poet Gary Snyder, *The Real Work: Interviews and Talks: 1964-1979* (New York: New Directions, 1980).

6 Gerard Manley Hopkins in his poem "God's Grandeur," says that in nature "lives the dearest freshness deep down things."

7 See Martin Buber, *I and Thou*, trans. Walter Kaufmann (New York: Charles Scribner's Sons, 1970).

8 For more on Eckhart, see Matthew Fox, ed., *Breakthrough: Meister Eckhart's Creation Spirituality in New Translation* (Garden City, NY: Doubleday, 1980). For the Tao as more like a seeing than an object of sight, see Smullyan, *The Tao is Silent*, chapter twenty-two: "Is God a Taoist?"

9 See chapters six and ten. Plato's comparison of the parts of the soul and the parts of the polis can be found in the *Republic*; the doctrine of the twelve officials can be found in the *Yellow Emperor's Classic of Internal Medicine* (*Huang Ti Nei Ching*).

10 See Frederick S. Perls, *Gestalt Therapy Verbatim* (Moab, Utah: Real People Press, 1969) and *The Gestalt Approach & Eye Witness to Therapy* (Palo Alto, CA: Science and Behavior Books, 1973).

11 For Transactional Analysis, see Eric Berne, *Games People Play: The Psychology of Human Relationships* (New York: Grove Press, 1964) and also his *What Do You Say After You Say Hello?* (New York: Bantam, 1973).

12 For Jung, see Joseph Campbell, ed., *The Portable Jung* (New York: Viking Press, 1971), especially, Part One. Note also Edward C. Whitmont, *The Symbolic Quest: Basic Concepts in Analytical Psychology* (New York: Harper and Row, 1973) and John A. Sanford, *The Invisible Partners* (New York: Paulist Press, 1980).

13 My approach here is wider than Kegan's. Compare Kegan's stage 4 with its emphasis on the questions: Who is in charge? How do I manage my many selves? See Kegan, *The Evolving Self*, chapter eight.

14 See Terrence, *Heauton Timoroumenos*, act I, scene 1.

15 Chief Seattle, Chief of the Dwarmish, upon surrendering his land to Governor Isaac Stevens in 1855. See *The Washington Historical Quarterly* 22, vol. IV (Oct. 1931), the Washington University State Historical Society, Seattle, Washington.

[16] See Raymond M. Smullyan, *The Tao is Silent*, chapter fourteen and passim.

[17] Consider, for example, *Analects*, IV: 10; XIV: 32; XVII: 8; XVIII: 8.

[18] See *Tao Te Ching*, chapter 38. For discussion, see my "Ethics in a Five Phase Framework," *Journal of Traditional Acupuncture*, Vol. IX, no. 2, Spring/Summer, 1987.

[19] See, for example, *Analects* VI: 30.

[20] Quoted from Ram Dass and Paul Gorman, *How Can I Help?*, p. 42.

[21] See, for example, the notion of Confucian reflection in Hall and Ames, *Thinking Through Confucius*; see the notion of *ch'eng* in the *Doctrine of the Mean*; see the frankly mystical tendencies of Mencius. On the Taoist side, see Henry Wei, *The Guiding Light*, on Lao Tzu. Consider also the mystical tendencies of Chuang Tzu, the schools of inner alchemy, the association of Taoism with the martial arts, and with Buddhism.

[22] I am more explicit than Legge in naming the two interpretations Confucian and Taoist.

[23] Legge trans., *Confucius*, with slight modifications.

[24] What I am calling the cultural domain, Thomas Berry calls "the pan-human." See Berry, *Affectivity*.

[25] See Bernard Lonergan, *Method in Theology*. See also Hall and Ames, *Thinking Through Confucius*, on learning. See also *The Doctrine of the Mean*, chapter twenty, and Wing-Tsit Chan's comment in *A Source Book*, p. 109: "The five steps of study, inquiry, thinking, sifting and practice could have come from John Dewey."

[26] Legge's note on text of Confucius in *The Great Learning*. See his *Confucius*, p. 356.

[27] For a like sentiment, see Socrates' prayer in the *Phaedo*.

[28] See *The Great Learning*, chapter seven, 2. Also note the effect of the opening of the *Chung-yung* (*Doctrine of the Mean*), on the heart before passions arise and the heart after passions arise.

[29] *The Great Learning*, chapter eight. Language modified for inclusiveness.

[30] I refer here to the four Confucian virtues: *jen* or human-heartedness; *yi* or appropriateness; *li* or the respect in seeing rituals in their depth; and *chih* or wise, ongoing learning.

[31] See Berry, *Affectivity*. Also see *Mencius*, IV B: 29.

PART FOUR

LIFE AS HEALING SERVICE

Returning to the Source

THE IMAGE: MOVING TO THE DEPTHS OF THE LAKE

Return one last time to the lake. Not to the lake seen between the heavens above and the earth below — the lake showing the cycles of energy. Not to the concentric circles on the surface of the lake — the lake showing the contexts for dwelling. Rather let us return to the lake as illustrating depth — to the surface of the lake, the mid-level of the lake and the depths of the lake.

Imagine that you are a ripple on the lake's surface. Aware that you are a ripple, you look around — perhaps to compare yourself to other ripples. "I am," you think, "quite a grand ripple — much stronger and more beautiful than those other puny, ugly ripples over there. And I am in a better section of the pond, more spacious, less crowded than other sectors." Such might be the thoughts of you, the ripple.

Now, release your identification with the surface ripple and descend down into the lake, to a depth midway between the surface and the bottom. Magically, you are able to breath normally. You feel peaceful here, as if you were lying on your back and looking up. You see the surface from below it. You see storms come and disturb the surface; rains come and alter the appearance of the surface; you see ice form and transform the surface water. You are an observer of the surface, but not identified with the surface. You are quite peaceful at this depth.

Imagine that once more you disengage, cease to identify with the mid-level (observing) self, and sink to the very bottom of the lake. It is darker here and fearful at first, more difficult to get your bearings. As you eventually relax into your new condition, you realize that you are, in a sense, all the water and all its manifestations. Also you perceive, for the first time, deeper, more subtle rhythms, longer cadences. You sense that the pond is connected to an ocean, vast beyond measure, and you are at one with its tides and seasons, its being and becoming.[1]

Such is the image for Part Four: life at the surface, in the middle, and at the very depth. The analogy is not to domains — contexts for dwelling; each domain could be considered a pond. The analogy here is rather to modes of consciousness — ways of knowing, ways of seeing and being.

The three modes of awareness — modes of understanding and relating to life — can be pictured in this fashion:

. Mode-Y (Surface, Automatic Mind)
.... o ....
. Mode-Z (Observing Self)

.... o ....
. Mode Omega (*Satori*; Enlightenment)

In Part Four, we shall explore life as healing presence. Healing presence is a way of knowing and a way of being. To appreciate the cycles of energy in each of the domains of dwelling, we are called to deeper modes of awareness. I shall correlate Confucius' narrow-minded person (in us) with my *mode-of-awareness-Y* and his large-minded person (in us) with my *mode-of-awareness-Z*.

The general features of *mode-Y* and *mode-Z* are compared in the following chart — according to Self-Awareness, Motivation, Psycho-Logic, and Action:

	Self Awareness	Motivation	Psycho-Logic	Action
	*	.	. Either-Or	.
	* Survival	. Reward/	. I'm right;	. Narrowly
MODE-Y	* mode/	. punishment;	. you're wrong.	. competitive,
	* Separate	. Praise/	. "Us vs. them."	. aggressive.
	* self	. blame	. For me to win,	. "Tit for tat"
	*	.	. you must lose.	. reactive
	*	.	. (seesaw)	.
———— O				
	* "Therapist,"	. "Serving	. Both-And	. Collaborative
	* healing	. the task"	. "Win-Win"	. *wu wei* -
MODE-Z	* mode/			. acting without
	* Observing,		. (Reframing	. causing
	* listening		. to move	. adverse
	* Self	.	. beyond dualism) .	reaction

MODE	*	*BEYOND DISTINCTIONS*		
OMEGA	*			

* * * * * * * * * * * * * * * * * * * *

Mode-Y is a state of automatic mind. This is our ordinary, often literalist, body-centered mode of consciousness. This is our surface or ego-dominated way of seeing and being. Here, we operate on "automatic pilot." In this state, we live much of our life.

When in this surface mode of awareness, we identify with a separate, survival self and we are acutely tuned to reward and punishment, praise and blame. We exist in a field of fear and desire. Our thinking is dualistic, "either-or" thinking — "I'm right; you're wrong; I'm justified; you're invalidated." Our loyalties tend to the tribal "us vs. them." We are quick to create enemies and scapegoats. Our "opinions" tend to be "tapes" — things we (and our crowd) have been saying over and over for years. Actions are also seen dualistically. In this frame of mind, I think of life as a seesaw — if I win, you lose; if you rise, I am diminished. Action is measured by consequences to me. Getting even is validated.

By contrast, *mode-Z* is like a state of awakened heart. More like meditative mind than full enlightenment, it is sometimes called the "observing self."[2] *Mode-Z* observes without imposing judgment, in the compassionate manner of a good therapist.

In *mode-Z*, we are motivated by what the Sufis call "serving the task."[3] The issue is not reward/punishment, but what is required by the nature of the task. *Mode-Z* seeks to move beyond the enemy mentality of "us vs. them." Its "psycho-logic" is to go beyond *either-or* dualism — to expand possibility, to reframe problems, to seek "win-win" (*both-and*) solutions, to inspire collaborative endeavors. Actions here flow out of a deep listening and an attunement to what is required. The mode of action is what Taoist call *wei wu wei* — to act by not-acting, to respond with a disarming spontaneity, to act without causing fruitless "tit for tat" reaction.

In *mode-Z*, we are able to see and take responsibility for our narrow identifications, constricting self-images and evasions. We see our "games" and those of others — not naively, but with some sense of how easily we and others are trapped by fear and desire. We have a capacity for empathy, and understand more of the shared human condition. We laugh at ourselves more easily and are more likely to forgive ourselves and others. Like the wise therapist or parent, we are able to hear what is said and unsaid, able to see what is needed at this time, in this situation. *Mode-Z* is thus a healing presence.

We can practice moving to mode-Z by accepting the following invitations:

1. Acknowledge the healing self
   (at mid-level — between surface and source).
2. Observe the process.
3. Serve the task.
4. Reframe dualisms.
5. Act collaboratively in *wu wei* fashion.

Notes

[1] In this meditative exercise, I elaborate upon a pond analogy in Arthur J. Deikman, *The Observing Self*, pp.103-04.

[2] See *ibid.*

[3] On serving the task, see Deikman, *The Observing Self*, chapter seven. Also see Alasdair MacIntyre, *After Virtue*, pp. 175-76.

CHAPTER FOURTEEN

A HEALING PRESENCE

The wild geese do not intend to cast their reflection.
The water has no mind to receive their image.
— *Zenrin Kushu*

Once upon a time — in a time much like our own, there lived a set of twins: a brother and a sister.[1]

From the beginning, both felt called to be healers. In their youth, a teacher came to them. Now, both are grown. They have been practicing the healing arts for some years.

One day, the sister said: "The way we see our art is far too limited. For very long now, I have thought of myself as one individual treating another individual. Now I see the limits of this view. Recently, I have read: *"The person is an 'individual' and an 'embeddual.'"*[2] I believe it is so. The person is an individual and an embeddual — embedded in a family."

"Excellent," said the brother. "Clearly, the true patient is the *family*. Let's bring the whole family in for treatment. Let's invent *family therapy*."

The brother was quite disappointed to learn that family therapy had already been invented. "Why wasn't I told?" he grumbled.

One day, the sister said: "Perhaps we are thinking in too small a fashion. Perhaps families too are embedduals — embedded in the web of rules and roles that constitute the Kingdom." (The sister loved to talk of things such as "the kingdom.")

Her brother was uncomfortable with such talk and ventured a

correction. "I believe you are thinking of institutions," he said — "institutions like corporations and colleges and churches and government agencies. We live in and under institutions in a modern nation state."

His sister nodded. "In earlier times, very many farmed the land. No longer is this how and where the work is done. Now we are ringed round with organizations."

"Excellent," said the brother. "Surely, the *institution* is the true patient. Let's bring the whole institution in for treatment. We can invent *institutional therapy*."

But something like institutional therapy had already been invented, and was being practiced by numerous consultants. "Why didn't someone tell me?" the brother muttered.

And so it went. The brother and sister paid attention to the *individual* who was also a *familial* who was also an *institutional*. However, life was no longer simple. An organization is too large to fit into a treatment room. Furthermore, the twins found that much of institutions is invisible. The institution is *people plus policies and procedures and power*. Yet institutions seemed to constitute "the real world," assimilating individuals to their purposes. "I sense something else," said the sister. "The major institutions seem less like machines, more like conscious organisms. They enchant their people with stories and symbols, myths and rituals. Individual organizations, networks of institutions, and nations live as in a drama and a dream. They sustain and reinforce the pattern of their culture."

"Excellent," said the brother. "Most assuredly, the true patient is the *culture*. Let's attend to the culture and invent *cultural therapy*."

Though no one flatly told the brother that cultural therapy had already been invented, a number of his friends thought that it had. One of his friends declared that prophets were cultural therapists, mentioning Amos and Martin Luther King, Jr. Another offered Socrates and the Greek playwrights as cultural therapists. A third spoke of Gandhi and Mother Teresa. A fourth mentioned Confucius and his sense of communal renewal through shared ritual. The brother was encouraged and wished to begin at once. But his sister showed reluctance.

"Perhaps," she said slowly, "we are still thinking in too small a fashion. Indeed, the kingdoms and the cultural epochs themselves seem to be a part of the planet earth. The planet earth behaves like a living, conscious organism."

"Excellent," said the brother. "There is no question; the *earth* is the true patient. Let us treat the earth and invent *earth therapy*."

The thought was, however, staggering. What place could accommodate the whole earth? Where would one stand to treat?

Ah, said the sister, suddenly struck by the great beauty and power of this insight. "Then all our work is world work. The earth is the *healer* as well as the *patient*. It is always a matter of 'Physician, heal thyself.' " She embraced her brother and felt herself embracing the earth.

A. On Healers and Patients

In my story, the brother speaks more in the tone of detached or separated knowing. The patient and the healer are experienced as separate. The sister speaks more in the tone of connected knowing. The patient and the healer are one.[3] Both perspectives are possible. We can "*relate to*" or *identify with* each of the domains.

In *relating to* the domains (especially the intermediary five), we experience them as other — as involving more than one individual, as being older than one lifetime, as shaped by structures and meanings not of our making. This is true: *they are not just us*. However, we can easily go on to think of "treating" friendships and family, institutions, cultures and the planet, as if they were *wholly other* than ourselves.

In *identifying with* the domains, we take responsibility for friendships and family, institutions and culture, and for the planet itself. *They are us*. In the spirit of the American psychologist, James Mark Baldwin, we can note that every genuine act of self-sacrifice is also self-enhancing.[4] We let go of a smaller center and reclaim a larger center. Of course, we are, in truth, *already and always* all the domains. We are part of the problem and part of the solution in each.[5]

Both the brother and sister began where we all tend to begin: in the personal and interpersonal domains. The patient is an individual and so is the healer. But this is far from the whole story. When I, as healer or patient, enter the treatment room, I bring with me all of the domains. *All the domains dwell in me*. I am all my emotions at the moment. I am all the key interpersonal experiences in my life thus far. I bring with me my parents and children. I am marked by my place in the network of institutions, by my nation and cultural epoch, by the history of humankind and by the evolution of all forms of life on this planet we coinhabit. All the domains dwell in me. I claim and disclaim and reclaim them. In this way, both patient and healer are "irreducibly relational."

Yet there is another insight here: *I dwell in all the domains*. I do not simply live my life alone — I am in relation with particular others; I exist in the generational time of family. I am advantaged or disadvantaged in my relationships to powerful institutions. I am conditioned by a collective culture with its understandings and misunderstandings, its insights and oversights, its genuine and distorted values. I confront a plurality of species and regions; I, along with others, encourage and discourage wholeness on the planet. Because the circles of life involve more than me alone and more than this moment or lifetime, change will have to occur both on personal and interpersonal levels, in familial arrangements and institutional structures, in shared cultural meanings and values, and in our collective sense of kinship with other times, other places, other species. The problems are partly in us and partly beyond us.

Who is the patient? In each treatment, we must decide which domains require attention.[6] It matters how and where we intervene. Yet the domains are patterns within patterns. When healing occurs in any domain, all will be affected.

The twins were expanding their awareness, learning that movement was possible within and among domains. But perhaps the sister voiced the most profound learning: *that the Earth or Nature itself is the primary healer*. What does this mean?

Taking earth as healer signals a shift in standpoints. Recall that the brother tended to separated knowing; the sister, to connected knowing. Yet whoever moves more deeply into the waters (into Awareness Z), begins to realize that certain "separations and connections" name phenomena in a dance at the surface. In *mode-Z*, we begin to glimpse that these separations and connections both arise from a *prior unity*. From the midpoint of the waters, we observe the surface dynamics and we sense that everything has roots in a deeper source. When we say that nature is the primary healer, we point to that source.

B. On the Way of Nature

Cycles of energy and *domains for dwelling* both belong to earth's story. Cycles stress the *ancient*, the *archetypal*, the *recurring*, the *similar*. Domains (with their associated timeframes) stress the *new*, the *surprising*, the *nonrepeating*, the *unique*. Both arise from the earth as learner/teacher. Both belong together and co-define what it means to come from prior unity — a unity that manifests itself in archetypal rhythms and common ancestry.

At times, earth's lessons seem simple: day and night, balance and imbalance, five basic elements or seasons of the year or seasons of a life, twelve functions within the body and within the kingdom. We see how separation, stuckness and starvations occur. We see how connection is available; how we can recontact life's deep motion; and how, collectively, we have all we need. At times, earth's lessons seem simple.

Yet when we acknowledge our method and recall the domains, more complexity appears. Earth's systems (cyclic and developmental) are refracted through cultural lenses. Each epoch reveals and conceals. Furthermore, we contain within us many layers from many cultural epochs. Patriarchal religion, technological medicine and new images of ecological wholeness arise from diverse epochs but coexist in the present time. We see nature through multiple, shifting, often contradictory lenses. We understand power as the institutional world shows us power. We understand kinship as family has taught us. The many voices within us oscillate between a view of nature as inferior, as mere matter to be used, and a view of nature as an elder teacher to be respected.[7]

Our modern epoch teaches that there is no privileged standpoint from which to speak of the way of Nature. There are, however two aids:

First, there is the process that theologian John S. Dunne calls "passing over and returning."[8] We have "passed over and returned" many times in moving between old and new, mystic and scientist, Eastern healer and Western therapist.

Second, there is meditative practice — movement from the surface to the mid-point and thence, at least darkly and obscurely, to the depth. Lao Tzu counsels us to let go of surface obstacles and return to a deeper nature; Confucius reminds us of the small-minded person and large-minded person in us. The movement from surface awareness (Y) to the observing self (Z) is a descent that invites us to healing service. It is time to review those lessons.

C. The Cyclic Patterns Revisited

Part Two of this book retold the ancient wisdom that undergirds traditional Chinese healing practices, how one circle unfolds in three stages: First, the circle appears inscribed with yin and yang, with rising and falling energy. Second, the yin-yang circle expands to show the five elements or phases. Third, the five elements become the five ministries and the twelve officials appear. The officials remind us of the functions for good health in body personal or body politic or body planetary. The chart that follows provides a reminder of these three differentiations, by showing yin-yang, five elements and six of the twelve officials. To emphasize the outward yang arc and the inward yin arc, I present three yang-side officials in masculine personae and three yin-side officials in feminine personae.[9]

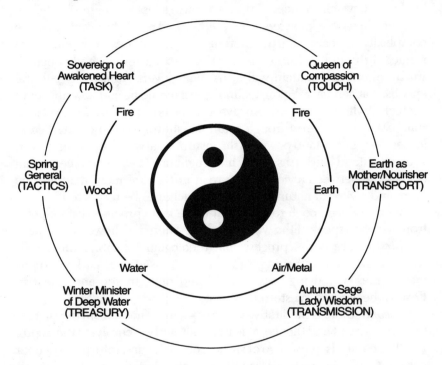

These energies — whether seen in the context of the two, five or twelve — can manifest imbalance, can show up as separation, stuckness, and starvation. Imbalances of these types can occur in ourselves moment by moment, in our friendships over a lifetime, in our families over generations, in our institutions over centuries, in our cultural dreams — epoch after epoch, and in the story of earth itself over aeons.

From this perspective, our work in each domain is one of:
  (i) recognizing separation and recovering the interconnection
     of life;
  (ii) recognizing stuckness and restoring the movement
     of life; and

(iii) recognizing starvation and returning to the sufficiency
   of life.

When we do these things, in whatever domain, we become a healing presence, an instrument of service. Let us look more closely at what is involved.

D. THE DOMAINS REVISITED

The domains are interconnected. Change is possible within a domain. Change is possible between domains. In fact, change anywhere will have some effect throughout. This is because the domains are patterns within patterns, nested contexts within nested time.

Suppose that we take a perspective in Z, at the mid-depth. Suppose we see the domains as concentric circles above us and sense a prior unity at the depth of life, below us. Such a viewpoint involves:

(i)   "serving the task" in each domain,
(ii) adopting a therapeutic mode of awareness in each domain,
(iii) reframing issues in each domain to move beyond dualisms,
(iv) stressing collaborative action in each domain.[10]

If we come to each domain in Awareness-Z, we shall see dualities above and affirm prior unity below. We shall see the cycles of energy in each domain and the unity expressed by the one source, one circle , one chi energy. We shall find a common story and common source in the timeframes of the domains. The planetary domain evokes the aeons of time in which earth developed, aeons stretching back to the birth of the universe itself. We are indeed born of stars! Furthermore, we share a home planet with many species, forms of life that are our elders. We are beginning to reclaim wonder, to discover a story that, as theologian Matthew Fox, would say, is large enough to include science, art and spirituality. Diversity appears under the sign of prior unity.

In the cultural domain, we find the home of the human — human meaning and value, story and symbol, worth and purpose, in the face of the death. We are beginning to prize the diverse myths and rituals that have guided the family of humankind in many places and epochs — learning anew to enter into those myths and rituals and to recover cross-cultural criteria for being human.[11] At the roots, diversity appears under the sign of prior unity.

Planetary and institutional domains have parallels, accenting space and organization. Institutions as self-sustaining organizations mirror the earth as a self-sustaining organization. Organizations call to mind task, teamwork, traditions of excellence, and trust. Perhaps the prime organizational task is to create the conditions for C.A.R.E. — for Collaborative And Respectful Existence — through which humans and other living things can grow, flourish, and contribute in turn.

Cultural and familial domains have parallels, accenting time and tradition. The family domain with its stories of generations mirrors the cultural domain with its story of humankind. Family scripts as well as cultural scripts can constrict or enlarge our thinking. Both stories remember ancestry and posterity.

Lastly, the personal and interpersonal domains call us to self-cultivation with its inquiry, sincerity, and rectification of heart; allow intimacy, disclosure and feedback; and make it possible for us to meet one another as very particular and very human. Self-cultivation and friendship both accent the irreducibly relational character of all human dwelling.

To repeat: in each of the domains, we seek to recognize and remedy separateness, stuckness and starvation. In each domain, we seek to reframe dualisms so as to serve the task therapeutically, so as to encourage collaborative action.

First, from *mode-Z*, we realize that *separateness is a symptom*, calling us to a balance of merging and emerging, society and solitude. Both "separation and connection" are surface events; both have a place when seen from an awareness of prior unity. Then, we might speak of separation as unique agency, and of connection as communal sharing.[12]

Second, from *mode-Z*, we realize that *stuckness is a symptom*, calling us to a balance of movement and rest. Both movement and rest are surface events; both have a place when seen from an awareness of prior unity. Then, we might speak of movement and rest as necessary to *the motion which is life itself*, a profound motion which lies beneath continuity and change.[13]

Third, from *mode-Z*, we realize that *starvation is a symptom*, calling us to a balance between scarcity (having too little) and satiation (having too much). Both "having little and having much" are surface events; both have a place when seen from an awareness of prior unity. Then, we might speak of sufficiency or satisfaction, of *satis-facere,* of making life "enough." Deeper yet, we might speak of a fullness and emptiness which are, in a paradoxical way, one and the same reality.[14]

E. Being a Healing Presence

Suppose we practice coming from prior unity — recalling the prior unity of both the archetypal cyclical energy and the common origins of the domains. Suppose we practice standing in the mid-level of awareness with its commitment to serving the task, to therapeutic awareness, to moving beyond "either-or," and to encouraging collaborative, noninterfering action. Then we are already practicing being a healing presence. In what follows, I simply wish to give Confucius and Lao Tzu a last word.

1. The Confucian Spirit

We have already seen the four standard Confucian virtues (the Four Beginnings —*ssu-tuan*), which become the Five Virtues (*wu-te*) when *hsin* (loyalty, trustworthiness) is added.[15] These virtues order attitude and action within each of the domains. They are:

JEN — Humanity, or human-heartedness. (The Chinese character combines the character for "person" and the character for the number "two.")

YI — Just Action, or, as Hall and Ames would have it, action appropriate to person-in-context.[16]

LI — Ritual Propriety, or, I would say, the ability to consider the conventional down to its roots and the discerning skill to bring ritual, courteous actions "back to life."[17]

CHIH — Wisdom, which is close to the sense of ongoing inquiry in *The Great Learning*.

HSIN — Loyalty or faithfulness or trustworthiness.[18]

Also, there are the five virtues, which have been called foundational or metaethical or anthropocosmic principles.[19] We might label these five as "cross-domain virtues." They are:

JEN	SHU	HSIAO	CHING	CH'ENG
Humanity	Reciprocity	Filial Piety	Reverence	Authenticity

Suppose, as a speculation, we arrange these five in a familiar pattern:

JEN
Humanity

CH'ENG   *SHU*   *CHING*
Authenticity   Reciprocity   Reverence

HSIAO
Filial Piety

These virtues apply to each domain and they allow us to see linkages between domains.

Within and between domains, Reverence (*Ching*) is needed. Reverence, like the exercise of the bow, teaches acknowledgment and manifests the quality of respect evidenced by the Autumn Sage who is First Minister.

Within and between domains, Filial Piety (*Hsiao*) appears. Such filial piety becomes an expanded notion of time, origins, ancestry — a quality of treasuring such as is exemplified by the Winter Minister of Deep Waters.

Within and between domains, Authenticity (*Ch'eng*) is called for — a quality of being true to the nested nature of each domain, a flexibility such as is displayed by the Spring General in protecting the conditions for growth.

Within and between domains, Repricocity (*Shu*) is seen — a quality of interconnection such as is shown by the Ministers of Earth's Bounty and its Distribution.

Within and between domains, Humanity or Human-Heartedness (*Jen*) is evoked — a quality of receptivity and commitment to nurture such as is manifest by the Sovereign of Awakened Heart. This, in particular, is what we humans as humans can bring to each domain. The virtue of humanity or humaness (*Jen*) appears on both lists of virtues, joining the work within domains to the work of unifying domains, and showing in both the centrality of awakened heart.

2. The Taoist Spirit

Meditative discipline and deep trust come together brilliantly in Lao Tzu's *Tao Te Ching*. As there is a wisdom of the body (or body-mind-spirit), which goes beyond the conscious ego, so the wisdom of the planet is more profound than our collective technological ego. Earth is the great teacher of the ecological age. "Ocean-Earth"—especially water—is the first manifestation of the mysterious Tao. In the words of Lao Tzu:

> The highest good is like water.
> Water gives life to the ten thousand things and does not strive.
> It flows in places men reject and so is like the Tao.[20]

The Taoist celebrates an emptiness beyond dualities. To rest in emptiness, to act out of emptiness, is the Taoist way. To rest in not-knowing, to act out of not-knowing, is the Taoist way.

Perhaps the Great Paradox might be stated thus: Everything is O.K. just as it is *and* everything is not O.K. just as it is. The O.K. and the not-O.K. appear in the manifest world, the world of dualities. How is it — if such a crazy question be allowed — "beneath" this world of O.K. *and* not-O.K.? Is wholeness or brokenness the fundamental reality? No doubt, the true master would not choose, would laugh aloud. If a beginner foolishly chose, would she or he not choose to regard everything as perfectly all right at the unmanifest depth, while the O.K. and not-O.K. appear in the manifest world? Such a resting place would be like reassuring a young child when, half-awakened from a nightmare, she calls out and her parents say: "Everything—including the nightmare — is perfectly all right."

The discipline of the Taoist way is more like a letting go than building up, more like stepping aside than competing, more like being stupid than being smart, more like having nothing than having something. Trust, in the Taoist manner, is a confidence that, at depth, life is wiser than I am. Deepening that trust *is* the Taoist discipline.

> The wise student hears of the Tao and practices it diligently.
> The average student hears of the Tao and gives it thought
>   now and again.
> The foolish student hears of the Tao and laughs aloud.
> If there were no laughter, the Tao would not be what it is.[21]

The Taoist, in doing the "work," is meditative, practices letting go, and comes to simplicity and silence.

Who can wait quietly while the mud settles?
Who can remain still until the moment of action?[22]

Taoists avoid "fixing" in two senses of that word:

First, Taoists avoid fixing things in the sense of repairing them. Life is a feature of organisms, not machines. Fixing applies to machines; healing applies to organisms. And if healing occurs, not we but nature is the agent of healing. At most, we support and remove barriers. We do not fix in the sense of repairing.

Second, Taoists avoid fixing things in the sense of stopping movement. Taoist practice involves an ongoing avoidance of *labeling*, for labeling *stops* movement and possibility. In holding to silence and stillness, in the respect and acknowledgment of worth, a space of possibility is revealed, which quite paradoxically allows change to arise.[23]

In this chapter, I have described a practice of standing in *mode*-Z and being aware of both the surface and the source. I have recalled the Confucian path of building up virtues and the Taoist path of releasing obstacles to return to simplicity. I have acknowledged separation and connection, rest and movement, simplicity and abundance as all arising from the one energy. I have noted that the domains are communities waiting to be consciously shared, waiting to become communions. They are also patterns in the void, fragments of emptiness, mirrors of mystery. This is what gives them their capacity to touch the spirit. We respond to this capacity with gratitude and "inner work." The "inner work" is only inner in that it is the spirit aspect "within" the domains/communities/ communions. All is potentially practice. All work is world work. All work is also cultural work and institutional work and familial work and friendship work and self-cultivational work.

What does it mean to be a healing presence in each of the domains? In the spirit of the *Tao Te Ching*, we might say:

In friendship, to be a listening.
In the family, to sense the needs of one's parents and one's children.
In work, to stand ever for the space of renewed possibility
    and creative collaboration.
In the culture, to speak and to be silent appropriately.

Ever to take Earth as one's teacher, and thus
let the Tao become manifest
in each of the ten thousand things
that rise and fall in its embrace.

Notes

1 This is a revised version of a story I presented at the fifth conference of the Traditional Acupuncture Institute, "Dwelling on the Earth," September 23, 1988. See my article: "Beyond the 'Skin-Encapsulated Ego'. . .," *The Journal of Traditional Acupuncture*, Vol. X, no. 1, Winter 1988-89, pp. 7-9.

2 See Robert Kegan, *The Evolving Self*, p. 116.

3 On separate and connected knowing (though in a more procedural mode than is present here), see Mary Field Belenky, Blythe McVicker Clinchy, Nancy Rule Goldberger and Jill Mattuck Tarule, *Women's Ways of Knowing: The Development of Self, Voice, and Mind* (New York: Basic Books, 1986), chapter six.

4 On self-sacrifice and the ideal self, see James Mark Baldwin, *Social and Ethical Interpretations in Mental Development* (New York: Macmillan, 1906).

5 This is a variant of Eldridge Cleaver's dictum, made famous in the 1960s: "If you are not part of the solution, you are part of the problem."

6 One can "collapse" domains — for example, by treating all problems as only personal or interpersonal, as if changing hearts alone would solve them. This overlooks the need for changes in policies and procedures. One can also "inflate" domains — for example, by treating everything as cultural or global while forgetting the interpersonal and familial. In one of T.S. Eliot's plays, it is said: "His problem was himself, but he called it Australia."

7 Recall chapter nine.

8 This has been a constant theme in Dunne's work. See, for example, John S. Dunne, *A Search for God in Time and Memory* (New York: Macmillan, 1969); *The Way of All the Earth* (New York: Macmillan, 1972) and *The House of Wisdom* (San Francisco: Harper and Row, 1985).

9 Some observations may be helpful: First, Sovereign is here masculine; Heart Protector as Consort, feminine. Earth's functions of distribution (spleen meridian) and digestion (stomach meridian) are again seen together as they are in chapter eight of the *Nei Ching*. I have explicitly given the First Minister the persona of Lady Wisdom and thought of her as a magical spirit woman

with shamanistic features. Second, yin and yang are always contextual. There is a context in which the six *zang* officials here presented (Heart, Heart Protector, Spleen, Lungs, Kidney and Liver Meridians) are all considered yang, namely, in relation to their accompanying *fu* officials (Small Intestine, Triple Heater, Stomach, Colon, Bladder and Gallbladder Meridians). In this context, the *zang* officials are considered yang and the *fu* officials are considered yin.

[10] See chart on Motivation, Awareness, Psycho-logic and Action for mode-Y and mode-Z, in the "Prologue to Part Four."

[11] On the importance of recovering a consensus on the criteria for being human, see Frederick Franck, *Being Human Against All Odds* (Berkeley, CA: Asian Humanities, 1991).

[12] David Bakan, in his book, *The Duality of Human Existence* (Boston: Beacon Press, 1966) speaks of "agency" and "communion." While I avoid identifying "communion-agency" too simply with "yin-yang," there are significant similarities between Bakan's insights and the point I am making here.

[13] See Kegan, *The Evolving Self*. I speak of separation/connection; stuckness/ movement; starvation/sufficiency. For a parallel, see Robert Jay Lifton and Eric Olson, *Living and Dying* (New York: Praeger, 1974), where they analyze the child's earliest imagery of life and death in terms of three sets of opposites: connection-separation; movement-stasis; integrity [wholeness, integration]- disintegration.

[14] In the Buddhist tradition, *sunyata* refers to an emptiness that is filled with possibility (what Gestalt psychologist Fritz Perls refers to as the "fertile void"). The companion term *tathata* refers to the "suchness" of things, to the vivid, unique particularity of each existing reality. Thus, after a near death experience, many report seeing, as if for the first time, the face of a beloved, tasting anew a glass of orange juice, smelling afresh the cool morning air. This vivid particularity of particulars is *tathata*. See also Trungpa, *Shambhala*, on *drala* — chapters twelve and thirteen.

[15] See Tu Wei-Ming, *Centrality and Commonality*, p. 57.

[16] See Hall and Ames, *Thinking Through Confucius*, pp. 83-110.

[17] See Fingarette, *Confucius*; also Hall and Ames, *ibid*.

[18] See my discussion of this in the domain of friendship.

[19] As mentioned in the notes to chapter nine, the phrase is Mircea Eliade's — combining "anthropos" (man or human) and "cosmos"; it is appropriated by Tu Wei-Ming. See Tu Wei-Ming, *Centrality and Commonality*, p. 102; also Berry, "Authenticity."

[20] *Tao Te Ching*, Feng and English trans., chapter eight.

[21] *Ibid.*, chapter forty-one.

[22] *Ibid.*, chapter fifteen.

[23] On change that is not forced, in addition to the works by Frederick Perls (already mentioned), see Joen Fagan and Irma Lee Shepherd, *Gestalt Therapy Now* (New York: Harper and Row, 1971).

RETURN TO THE SOURCE

When the ten thousand things
are viewed in their one-ness,
we return to the Origin
and remain where we have always been.
— Seng-Ts'an[1]

What does it mean to return to the source — especially when we have the domains in view? What does it mean to return to the source of one's self, one's friendships, one's family? To return to the source of one's institutions and professions, national heritage and cultural epoch, species history and planetary place? To return to the source of the Great Pattern, of Life as Mystery, of the Tao?

In this section, I answer this question by way of a meditation on the Ten Oxherding Pictures. The Ten Oxherding Pictures are a mode of presenting the process of enlightenment. Before the twelfth century A.D., six or eight pictures were used. In the twelfth century, the Chinese Zen master, Kuo-an Shih-yuan, is credited with adding two more pictures, bringing the number to ten.[2] The drawings and commentary attributed to this Zen master are now standard.

My commentary shall introduce several new themes.

(1) The Oxherding Pictures are usually seen as the process of individual enlightenment; I shall treat them in the communal context of the domains.

(2) The Oxherding Pictures are usually treated one at a time; I shall consider five phases, taking the pictures two at a time.

(3) The Oxherding Pictures — arising from the Zen tradition — are closer to Taoist than Confucian themes; I shall walk with both guides. As

a speculation, I shall correlate one of the Confucian metaethical or interdomain virtues with each of the five phases.[3]

(4) The ninth Oxherding Picture is called "Return to the Source." In this meditative chapter, I shall look at returning to the source in five phases: (a) return to the unknown, (b) return to the real, (c) return to the heart, (d) return to time and the timeless, and (e) return to the world.

A. THE FIRST PHASE: RETURN TO THE UNKNOWN

In the Oxherding series, *the first picture is "Seeking the Ox"; the second, "Finding the Tracks of the Ox."*

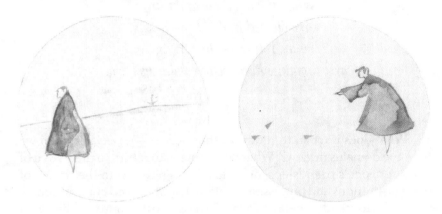

The ox is taken to be one's original nature or total mind. At first, the ox is seen from a dualistic perspective. There is the ox and there is myself. So seen, the ox and myself appear as two, somewhat as *mode-Z* and *mode-Y* are seen as two. At first, standing in *mode-Y*, I simply realize that something is missing, that I am not at one with the deepest stirrings of my heart and mind. This is perhaps an intuition of something more — symbolize it as "Z." The "something more" appears as a lack, an emptiness, a loss.

The earliest awakening is an awakening to our being lost, an acknowledgment of our own ignorance, an admission that we do not know how to proceed. The cry is universal. With Socrates, the beginning is an admission of our unknowing. In Dante, the acknowledgment of being lost opens the *Divine Comedy*. "In the midst of the journey of our life, I came to find myself in a dark wood where direct escape was blocked." From India comes a sense of discovering that we are in Avidya

— a deep and destructive ignorance of who we are. The Oxherding Pictures begin with the oxherder experiencing the ox as lost; *in the first picture, the oxherder is seeking the ox.*

Later, the oxherder will realize that our fundamental unity is never lost. Like a man with his glasses on his head looking for his glasses, the basic unity is as near as he is to himself. The poignant irony is expressed in lines like these:

We are like those who,
    immersed in water,
stretch out their hands,
    begging for a drink.
          — Seppo

We have one moon,
    clear and unclouded.
Yet we are lost
    In the darkness of the world.
          — Ikkyu[4]

Of course, this is not what is experienced at the start. The ox appears to be lost; it is only intuited, and when named, it is already conceived as other, as two. The experience of being lost may surface in any of the domains: in solitude, friendship, family, work, culture or earth.

The second picture is "Finding the Tracks of the Ox." We spy the footprints of the ox in the spiritual and artistic traditions. In Neolithic times, the footprints are the symbols of the Great Goddess. In tribal, shamanic times, the footprints are the lived kinship expressed by a Chief Seattle. In classical times, the footprints are the written scriptures or classics. Throughout the technological age, the footprints are carried by a spirituality that is often secular, finding guidance in science and committed to human rights and human dignity.[5] In the emerging eco-logical age, we are seeking a convergence, a way of being attuned to footprints in all places and times, a story large enough for science, spirituality and art to dwell together.

Throughout this work, I have drawn on the classics of ancient China. I have presented the footprints of the ox in both Taoist and Confucian texts. I have, at the same time, acknowledged that what is seen through the two perspectives of Lao Tzu and Confucius are insights which also appear in the mystical strands of other great traditions and in each epoch.

However, as the tracks of the ox are multiple (arising from many communities), so too the awakening is not confined to an isolated me. I can awaken in my friendships and family. I can find traces in the exemplars of excellence in my profession and in my culture. I can find the tracks in my kinship with humanity and in my wider kinship with all the living beings in nature.

More surprising still, I can sometimes glimpse the tracks of the ox through the pain, suffering and sorrow of the world. The great figure of Kwannon is "She who hears the cries of the world." The cries of friendships betrayed, families wasted, institutional power without justice, the pain of cultures that disempower, the suffering of species on the global plane. These too are tracks of the ox. What does it mean to return to the source here?

It is to return to unknowing, to mystery, to inquiry.

When confronting the suffering side of the domains, we experience grief and loss. We are hurt, saddened; our hearts are bruised; our hopes shattered. We descend to the waters chaotic, and fear we shall drown.[6]

Here is the return to unknowing. No recipes. Nothing but presence to the painful situation. What is needed to proceed? Certainly, acknowledgment of worth, remembrance of what still surrounds and supports us, refusal to count the present disaster as all we are. Then, we respond as appropriately as we can — gently, recognizing our own fragility and that of others; tentatively, recognizing the uniqueness of persons and institutions at particular times in their individual and collective lives.

While contemplating the first two pictures, we think of the metaethical virtue *ching* — a reverence in the face of the recurring and unrepeatable events of life. Always, at beginnings, we need reverence, respect, acknowledgment. Thus did we begin this book — with the bow, with a sense of acknowledgment. What we trust in such moments has no simple name. Out of such mystery, with reverence and trust, we inquire into life anew. Such inquiry is highly experimental, highly attuned to disclosure and feedback.

What is lost and what gives evidence that it can be found? It is the way — heard and unheard as friend speaks to friend, seen and unseen, as family members interact, revealed and concealed in institutions and cultures, known and unknown, as species contacts species. As in the *Great Learning*, return to the unknown, to mystery, initiates inquiry. There is something to seek, a more excellent way to travel. And the seeking is a matter of life and death — the life or death of ourselves, our relationships, our families, our institutions, our nations and our planet.

B. The Second Phase: Return to the Real

In the Oxherding Series, *the third picture is "First Glimpse of the Ox"; the fourth, "Catching the Ox."*

At this juncture, we catch sight of the ox. Not only do we have the testimony of others (the footprints), we experience our nature itself. Our true nature is glimpsed, but it appears unruly and untamed. The Source is everywhere, in every action, every thing or process. We have glimpsed that it is so. Yet the experience is fleeting, and then we are returned to the flattened everyday. At this point, we feel the trap of twoness and may ask: Will the real me stand up? Perhaps the experience is that of St. Paul: "The good that I will, that I do not do. The evil which I wish to avoid that I am drawn to. . . . O unhappy person that I am!"[7] Here twoness is experienced as dualism of senses and spirit, of body and mind, or of what we are and what we could/might/should be. Put differently, we experience seeing in a surface manner and in a deeper manner. We experience some moments of unity with friend or spouse. We know how it can be . . . . then lose it. We grasp how our family might be, how our institution or profession might make its contribution, how our culture could empower, how the earth could again heal us. Then we lose the experience, doubt the possibility, and wonder "what is real?"

At times, we move through the doubleness. Some oppositions call for harmony, as when we glimpse a deeper unity between East and West, sagely and kingly, Taoist and Confucian. Some pairs point to development: as when we desire to move from the inferior person-in-us (*hsiao jen*) to the superior person-in-us (*chün tzu*), or from the hegemon (*pa*) to the true king (*wang*). Some tensions require constant balancing and rebalancing, in a fashion of a tightrope walker, as when, for example, we know our children need both order and freedom, or when we prize both equality and excellence. In these matters, there can be no once-and-for-all recipe.[8] We feel conflicting claims within and among domains, and these require constant adjustments. *To catch the ox is to hold the paradox* — in whatever domains we experience it.

The metaethical virtue for this phase is *ch'eng* — authenticity, honesty, sincerity, realization. Here we see the second step of *The Great Learning*. In order to have inquiry into life, an unswerving honesty is needed. In fact, that honesty was needed to recognize our ignorance, our lostness. Honesty touches the real; there is a sense of kinship with what matters. We remember what we have felt as real, what we have given or let go of that results in the real. The inquiry begun now becomes a process of realization, making real, realizing the friendship, the family, the service of the kingdom, the archetypal rites, the interspecies kinship.

Honest inquiry is open-ended and involves bringing to light what is left out, acknowledging light and darkness, clarity and confusion, the front and back of the hand, the familiar and unfamiliar, what we expect and what arises to surprise us. To know what to say and what to leave unsaid, when to act and when to delay action, and to adapt constantly to ongoing feedback — these are the skills needed to deal in the *both-and* world. Any harmony here is provisional. Like a tightrope walker, we move by balancing, unbalancing, rebalancing. The struggle is to affirm both *mode-Y* and *mode-Z*, to affirm ideal and defect, in the midst of life. While the ox and self are experienced as two, struggle is inevitable. As the Hindu saying puts it: "Where there is other, there is fear." To catch the ox is perhaps to hold onto both poles of the polarities; so seen, they appear as tensions.

C. THE THIRD PHASE: RETURN TO THE HEART

In the Oxherding series, the fifth picture *is "Taming the Ox"; the sixth, "Riding the Ox Home."*

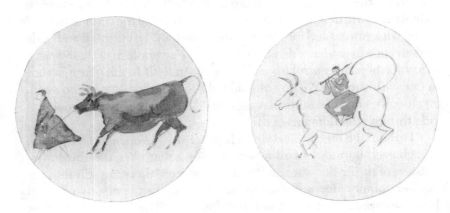

Think of the heart prior to the passions of life — a state of quietude. Think of the heart engaged in life, prompted by likes and dislikes, angers and enthusiasms, loves and betrayals, joy and depression, self-doubt and celebration, loss and gain, letting go and beginning anew.

The heart awakens in the midst of each domain under the influence of allurement.[9] We are drawn to our friends and become angry at those who would harm them. The heart awakens in recognition of the intergenerational gifts and wounds; awakens to institutional justice and injustice. We are drawn to the ideals of our cultural heroes and heroines. We awaken to discover what the culture reveres and despises, rewards and represses, what it barely tolerates and what it cannot even hear. The heart awakens in the midst of planetary seasons and cycles, in the midst of bioregions and forms of life familiar there, in the midst of pollution, environmental exploitation and species-extinction.

The awakened heart is tender, vulnerable, suffused with a bitter-sweet sense of both the suffering and the glory that life brings.[10] No longer in oscillation, unskillfully trying to remember *both-and*, the awakened heart has reframed even this issue. It is no longer yanked up and down by gain and loss, no longer seduced into praising and blaming, no longer having its identity tied up with right and wrong. The awakened heart sees through the dualism; even *mode-Z* and *mode-Y* dwell together. As is evident in meditation, the observing self is compassionate and at ease with the content that moves ceaselessly through the mind-space. Better yet, the awakened heart *is* that space in which dissolution of form is also possibility of renewal. This is the taming of the ox.

When the ox is tamed, we are at one with our body-mind-spirit. When the storm quiets, we are at Eliot's "still point of the turning world." Here, background and foreground are copresent. Here, mind and body become one as evidenced in the centaur-like symbolism of ox and rider in a union beyond controlling and being controlled. In this phase, we are at one with ourself. We do not hold tight to the reins; there is no need. At ease, we take up a flute; playing music, enjoying the countryside, we ride through the domains of life.

Perhaps the metaethical virtue here is *jen* — an enlarged humanity, an achieved harmony of all aspects of our being. We see this in the masters of the arts of war and the arts of peace;[11] there is a stillness, yet neither inquiry nor authenticity are lost. In fact, persons of deep humanity appear more alert and alive than ever. The *Tao Te Ching* gives us a wondrous picture of this unity at the existential level.

> The ancient masters were subtle, mysterious,
> profound, responsive.
> The depth of their knowledge is unfathomable.
> Because it is unfathomable,
> All we can do is describe their appearance.
> Watchful, like persons crossing a winter stream.
> Alert, like those aware of danger.
> Courteous, like visiting guests.
> Yielding, like ice about to melt.
> Simple, like uncarved blocks of wood.
> Hollow, like caves.
> Opaque, like muddy pools.
>
> Who can wait quietly while the mud settles?
> Who can remain still until the moment of action?
> Observers of the Tao do not seek fulfillment.
> Not seeking fulfillment, they are not swayed by
> desire for change.[12]

The Oxherding Pictures could indeed end here, at picture six. The struggle is over; music and harmony mark the mood. We experience a serene gaze, an undisturbed presence, a fresh breeze.

In the T'ang period, the Zen master Po-chang Huai-hai (A.D. 720-814) was asked about the Buddha (the awakened nature). "It is like seeking an ox while riding on it," he replied. Of what use, then, was such a "finding" of what had always been? "It is like going home riding on it," was the reply.[13]

When the space of awakened heart opens, in whatever domain, "it is like going home."[14] One can say that judgments cease, or one can say that all is clearly and compassionately seen. Such *seeing to the core of our humanness* is itself a love beyond love and hate.

> Riding free as air the rider buoyantly comes home
> through evening mists in wide straw-hat and cape.
> Wherever he may go he creates a fresh breeze,
> while in his heart profound tranquillity prevails.[15]

When we are at one in our relationships, in our intergenerational family, in our institutions as communities, in our national heritage, in our global citizenship, then we come home to them, creating a fresh breeze of wholeness, of possibility, of profound tranquillity.

D. THE FOURTH PHASE: RETURN TO TIME AND THE TIMELESS
In the Oxherding Series, *the seventh picture is "Ox Forgotten, Self Alone"; the eighth, "Both Ox and Self Forgotten."*

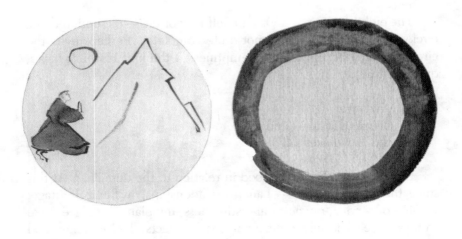

When the awakened heart stands courageously in life, when the domains are seen at their depth as communions, then the ox is forgotten. The oxherder is in his cottage, at home. The ox is nowhere in sight. There is no twoness here.

Some say the ox is Mind. If so, there are at least four aspects to distinguish: the two models of the mind (*modes* Y and Z) and the the two ways in which these models can be considered (dualistically, nondualistically). Dualistically seen, the Mind is unruly and needs to be tamed. At first, when we begin to meditate, we are only conscious of our chatter, which we try to eliminate by "striving." However, the chattering "monkey-mind" and its deep ground are not two, as we may discover. Nondualistically considered, the mind is literally "seen through." It disappears. However, a remnant may remain. A sort of echo of dualism. How spiritual I am! How thoroughly I have arrived! This may be spirituality's last temptation — to be, in Frederick Franck's phrase, "Zennier than thou," to be caught in what Trungpa calls "spiritual materialism."[16] Because this echo remains, we move on further — from picture seven to picture eight.

The next stage occurs when every belief, every accomplishment, every project that sustained us — when all, even what we have made our religion, falls away. Suddenly, there is nothing to grasp and nowhere to stand and no one but the emptiness. Here "both ox and self are forgotten." This is the Great Doubt, the Dark Night, the letting go of "not less than everything." At the same time, it is a deeper "going home," an ecstatic at-one-ment with the emptiness/fullness (*sunyata/tathata*) of existence.

The eighth picture — "Ox and Self Forgotten" — is rendered as a circle, spontaneously drawn, not quite complete. Perhaps even the circle is fading into pure white emptiness. I think of Hashin's haiku, quoted earlier:

> No sky at all;
> no earth at all — and still
> the snowflakes fall. . . . [17]

How is this to be understood in relation to the domains? At this stage, there is no twoness — I am my relationships, my family heritage, my line of service, my cultural distinctness, my planetary place. Like Indra's net, each jewel is precious and each reflects all. Uniqueness and universality are not at odds. I realize the timeless in time, the present in which all time resides.

When we experience this, we realize it is not the "passing present" of stream of consciousness, the distracted one-thing-after-another. Rather we experience a present and presence that has been tutored by the alertness of inquiry, the single-mindedness of honest recognitions, the embrace of the awakened heart. Here timely action and timeless contemplation fuse. What thought is there of one's true nature? Even spirituality in the self-conscious, self-inflating sense is left behind.

I would place here the metaethical virtue of *hsiao* — filial piety. I think of "filial piety" in its vastness, expanded to include a felt sense of origin. From the cosmic void, the great beginning, the forming of elements and planets and lifeforms through the human story in all epochs to our present biocentric/ecocentric awareness, such a sense of heritage intensifies and dignifies everything. Among the officials, this vast remembrance is held by the Master of Deep Waters.

From this perspective of time and origin, I also see the forms of human organization, the kingdoms that cradle life and the kingdoms that poison life. I see the forms of birthing and initiating the young. I see my friends and those I had not the skill or wisdom to reach. All have place in the pregnant present that births them continuously. Such a sense of origins sees the Tao in all the unfolding, in all gifts and wounds, ample in resources, silent enough to hear where the hurts are, spacious in possibility. What has come before and what is arising now combine artistically to suggest a future — the appropriate word, the generous act, the healing stillness.

Before the twelfth century, the Oxherding sequence ended here — with the eighth picture. To end here — in a Oneness where self and others disappear — is complete and incomplete. So thought the twelfth-century Chinese Zen master who is credited with adding two additional pictures. Before considering the final two pictures, I wish to reflect for a moment on completions that are also incomplete.

Consider the Oxherding sequence as presented, taking the pictures in pairs:

Pictures 1 and 2 — "Seeking the Ox" and "Glimpsing the Footprints" — bring a completion; this is the condition of belief that inspires Reverence (*ching*) and enacts acknowledgment.

Pictures 3 and 4 — "Seeing the Ox" and "Taking Hold of the Ox" — bring a completion; they move to the experiential but dualistic level.

They require of us *authenticity* (honesty, sincerity, single-mindedness —*ch'eng*) to transcend "either-or" and begin the practice of "both-and."

Pictures 5 and 6 — "Taming the Ox" and "Riding the Ox Home" — bring a completion; body and mind return to an organismic unity that expands *human-heartedness* (*jen*).

Steps 7 and 8 — "Ox Forgotten, Self Alone" and "Both Ox and Self Forgotten" — bring a completion; we sense the timeless in time and return to the origin where heritage intersects with here and now. Filial Piety (*hsaio*) returns to origins and expands to embrace all our kin. Surely this is a completion lacking nothing. And yet the twelfth-century Zen master did not "add legs to a snake" when he suggested two additional pictures. These two additional pictures bring a powerful reminder to our age.

E. THE FIFTH PHASE: RETURN TO THE WORLD

In the Oxherding series, *the ninth picture is "Returning to the Source"; the tenth, "Entering the Marketplace with Helping Hands."*

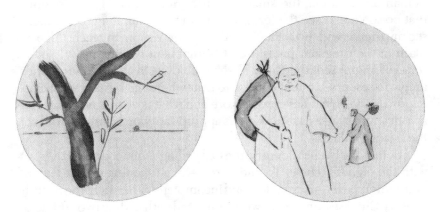

"Returning to the Source" is illustrated not with the iconographic circle, but by a scene of nature: rocks, plum blossoms, bamboo. In light of the domains, this takes on a special significance. The source here is the planetary domain, the communion of all beings, living and nonliving. This is the world that reflects the Tao, the world pristine, our ancestral world sustained still by species and cycles not of our making.

The oxherder is not in the picture, but the commentary states: "He observes the waxing and waning of life in the world while abiding unassertively in a state of unshakable serenity." There is no "this world" and "another world." The waxing and waning are not illusion but the Source manifesting itself. "Why then is there need to strive for anything? The waters are blue, the mountains are green."[18]

Indeed, there is no one to observe; only the rising and falling of the ten thousand things, which include all that we are. This is why the accompanying poem speaks of the oxherd as "now blind and deaf." What need is there to remove nature from nature? "Streams meander on of themselves, red flowers naturally bloom red."

And then comes the tenth picture: of the oxherd, looking fat like a Buddha, in the marketplace of the world. The commentary notes: "Even the wise cannot find him. . . . He goes his own way, making no attempt to follow the steps of earlier sages. Carrying a gourd, he strolls into the market; leaning on his staff, he returns home. He leads innkeepers and fishmongers in the Way of the Buddha."[19]

The accompanying poem proclaims:

> Barechested, barefooted, he comes into the market place.
> Muddied and dust-covered, how broadly he grins!
> Without recourse to mystic powers,
> > withered trees he swiftly brings to bloom.

If there is a metaethical virtue here, surely it is *shu* — a reciprocity that links all beings. The earth is here — humus, humility, humor. "How broadly, he grins!" Humor has the last word; it bursts open even the Golden Rule. What was at the kernel remains — a kinship beyond anything any of us do or fail to do, a reciprocity arising out of our primary connectedness.

The Sufi poet, Rumi, said: "There is a field, beyond right and wrong. Let's meet there."[20] The awakened one walks in the field beyond right and wrong, beyond praise and blame, walks through the dusty world bestowing blessings without a thought of doing or not doing. The field of Rumi's poem is the natural world, the world of the previous picture. We return to the world through the domains — from the planetary to the cultural. Through the cultural to the institutional. Now we are in the marketplace of the world. Our family story intersects here; our friendships arise in the midst of it all. And it matters greatly how asleep or awake we are.

"Returning to the Source" and "Entering the Marketplace with Helping Hands" — throughout our life we cycle them. In every domain or communion, we find them. It is said there are eighty thousand ways for us to fall asleep, and the sage knows eighty thousand ways to wake us up. One of the sages, Lao Tzu, says simply:

"The motion of the Tao consists in returning . . ."

Notes

1 Quoted in Nancy Wilson Ross, *The World of Zen*, p. 271. See also Frederick Franck, *Echoes from the Bottomless Well* (New York: Random House Vintage, 1985), p. 91.

2 Here, I follow the presentation in Philip Kapleau, *The Three Pillars of Zen* (Boston: Beacon Press, 1967), pp. 301-13. For an alternative interpretation of the pictures, see Willard Johnson, *Riding the Ox Home* (Boston: Beacon Press, 1982).

3 For a brief discussion of these virtues (called foundational or metaethical or anthropocosmic or interdomain virtues), see chapter fourteen.

4 Both poems are to be found in Frederick Franck, *The Book of Angelus Silesius*, p. 58.

5 For a strand of mysticism within science, see Ken Wilber, ed. *Quantum Questions: Mystical Writings of the World's Great Physicists* (Boulder, CO: Shambhala, 1984) and, for the humanist tradition, see, for example, the eighteenth- and nineteenth-century philosophers from Kant to Marx, and from Locke to Mill.

6 For early Taoist notions of chaos, see N. J. Girardot, *Myth and Meaning*.

7 See St. Paul, Epistle to the Romans, 7:19-24. Modified for inclusive language.

8 E. F. Schumacher calls these issues "divergent problems," see his *Guide For the Perplexed*, chapter ten.

9 On the notion of allurement as a cosmic force, see Brian Swimme, *The Universe is a Green Dragon*.

10 See Trungpa, *Shambhala*, chapter three: "The Genuine Heart of Sadness."

11 The martial arts include, as a sample, Tai Chi, Kung Fu, archery, and sword. The arts of peace include, as a sample, music, calligraphy, flower arranging, tea ceremony.

¹² *Tao Te Ching*, Feng and English trans., chapter fifteen. Modified for inclusive language.

¹³ See frontispiece of Willard Johnson, *Riding the Ox Home*. See also Daisetz Teitaro Suzuki, *Essays in Zen Buddhism: First Series* (New York: Grove Press, 1949/1961), Essay VIII.

¹⁴ On the theme of going home, see Dianne M. Connelly, *All Sickness is Homesickness*.

¹⁵ See commentary poem for picture six, Kapleau, *The Three Pillars*, p. 307.

¹⁶ See Chogyam Trungpa, *Cutting Through Spiritual Materialism* (Boulder, CO: Shambhala, 1973).

¹⁷ See chapter five, footnote 4.

¹⁸ This and the previously quoted sentence come from the ancient commentary. See Kapleau, *The Three Pillars*, p. 310.

¹⁹ *Ibid.*, p. 311.

²⁰ This rendering is how I remember the opening of the quatrain. For a more scholarly translation, see John Moyne and Coleman Barks, trans. *Open Secret: Versions of Rumi* (Putney, Vermont: Threshold Books, 1984), Quatrain no. 158.